From Dust We Walk Together

From Dust We Walk Together
© 2026 Kay Dennis. All rights reserved.

No part of this book may be reproduced or transmitted in any form or by any means—electronic, mechanical, photocopying, recording, or otherwise—without the prior written permission of the author, except in brief quotations used in reviews or articles.

Scripture quotations are from the New Revised Standard Version Bible, copyright © 1989 by the Division of Christian Education of the National Council of the Churches of Christ in the United States of America. Used by permission. All rights reserved.

ISBN: 979824199062
Cover design: Kay Dennis
Interior design and layout: Kay Dennis

10 9 8 7 6 5 4 3 2 1
First Edition
Printed in the United States of America

For permissions or correspondence, contact:
Kay Dennis
Kay.dennis@mail.com

Kay Dennis

Dedication

For all who enter the wilderness—
not to escape the world, but to love it more deeply.
For the weary souls who keep showing up—
to pray, to serve, to hope again.
For the Church that still gathers—
in sanctuaries and living rooms,
around kitchen tables and hospital beds,
beneath steeples and under open skies.
For every soul who has kept the faith
when the world grew quiet,
who has prayed through the ache of distance,
who has carried light for another
when their own flame was small.
For those who have felt the dust on their foreheads
and the weight of the world in their hearts,
yet still choose compassion over despair.
For the Church that remembers we are never
    alone—
not in our fasting, not in our hunger,
not in our dying, not in our rising.
And most of all for the God
who meets us in the wilderness,
walks beside us in the shadows,
and turns even dust into glory.

From Dust We Walk Together

Dedication Prayer

Gracious and Merciful Lord,
You formed us from the dust
and breathed into us the breath of life.
As we enter this holy season of Lent,
make these words a dwelling place for Your Spirit.

Bless every reader who turns these pages—
the searching, the sorrowful, the steadfast, the uncertain.
Let each reflection draw them nearer to Your heart
and nearer to one another.

May this book be more than ink and paper;
may it become a companion on the road to the cross,
a lantern in the wilderness,
a gentle reminder that Your love endures beyond death
and that no dust is ever forgotten by You.

Through Jesus Christ our Lord,
who leads us from ashes to Easter light.
Amen.

Kay Dennis

Spiritual Epigraph

We begin as dust,
each marked by loss and longing,
each carrying what we cannot heal alone.

God meets us not only in silence,
but in the sound of footsteps beside us—
in shared bread, shared ashes,
shared hope.

From dust we are formed.
By grace, we walk together.

From Dust We Walk Together

Kay Dennis

Preface

Lent begins with a reminder we all share: you are dust. The words are spoken to each of us personally, yet they are never spoken in isolation. We hear them while standing shoulder to shoulder, marked with the same ash, named by the same truth. From the very first day, Lent insists that repentance is communal before it is individual.

Too often, the spiritual life is framed as a solitary endeavor—private disciplines, inward reflection, personal resolve. Lent certainly asks us to look honestly at our own lives. But Scripture tells a deeper story alongside that work: God forms a people, not a collection of isolated seekers. We confess together. We fast together. We return together.

From Dust We Walk Together follows the Lenten journey from Ash Wednesday through the First Sunday of Easter, tracing the slow, necessary work of returning as a community shaped by grace. These devotionals are written for those who know that faith is not always strong, repentance not always neat, and hope not always immediately felt. Some days, belief must be carried by another. Some days, prayer is spoken on borrowed strength.

This book makes room for the shared weight of the season—for grief that lingers, for weariness that accumulates, for questions that do not resolve quickly. It does not rush the wilderness or soften the truth of the cross. Instead, it honors the long road of faith, trusting that God meets us not only in personal devotion, but in the presence of one another.

Whether these pages are read alone, in small groups, or within the life of a parish, they are offered as companions for the journey. Lent is not a test of endurance or spiritual achievement. It is a path of honesty, humility, and hope—one we were never meant to walk alone.

We are dust. And still, by grace, we walk together—toward the cross, toward the empty tomb, toward the God who binds us to one another on the way.

Kay Dennis

TABLE OF CONTENTS

Dedication _____ iii

Spiritual Epigraph _____ v

Preface _____ vii

Introduction: Together in Repentance _____ xv

Ash Wednesday — Marked as One Body _____ 1

Thursday after Ash Wednesday — The Dust We Share _____ 5

Friday after Ash Wednesday — Community of the Penitent _____ 9

Saturday after Ash Wednesday — Learning to Kneel Together _____ 13

The First Sunday of Lent — The Wilderness We Don't Face Alone _____ 17

Looking Ahead — Together in Trust _____ 21

Monday after the First Sunday of Lent — Nicodemus by Night _____ 23

Tuesday after the First Sunday of Lent — The Tent of Abraham _____ 27

Wednesday after the First Sunday of Lent — Faith Between Friends _____ 31

Thursday after the First Sunday of Lent — Covenant as Relationship ___ 35

Friday after the First Sunday of Lent — Born of Spirit, Born Together ___ 39

Saturday after the First Sunday of Lent — Trusting in the Dark ___ 43

The Second Sunday of Lent — Lifted Eyes, Shared Hope ___ 47

Monday of the Third Week of Lent — The Well at Noon ___ 51

John 4:5–15 (NRSV) ___ 51

Tuesday of the Third Week of Lent — Thirst for Understanding ___ 55

Wednesday of the Third Week of Lent — When Thirst Becomes Prayer ___ 59

Thursday of the Third Week of Lent — The Song of the Parched ___ 63

Friday of the Third Week of Lent — The Table in the Desert ___ 67

Saturday of the Third Week of Lent — The Well Revisited ___ 71

The Third Sunday of Lent — Streams in the Desert ___ 75

Looking Ahead — Together in Light _____ 79

Monday of the Fourth Week of Lent — Eyes Opened at Emmaus _____ 81

Tuesday of the Fourth Week of Lent — Light for the Blind _____ 85

Wednesday of the Fourth Week of Lent — Carried into the Light _____ 89

Thursday of the Fourth Week of Lent — Light in Unexpected Places _____ 93

Friday of the Fourth Week of Lent — When the Light Exposes Us _____ 97

Saturday of the Fourth Week of Lent — Reflections of the Light _____ 101

The Fourth Sunday of Lent — Walking as Children of the Light _____ 105

Looking Ahead — Together in Hope _____ 109

Monday of the Fifth Week of Lent — The Grain of Wheat _____ 111

Tuesday of the Fifth Week of Lent — The Valley of Dry Bones _____ 115

Wednesday of the Fifth Week of Lent — Those Who Wait for the Lord _____ 119

Thursday of the Fifth Week of Lent — A Future and a Hope _____ 123

Friday of the Fifth Week of Lent — Those Who Sow in Tears _____ 127

Saturday of the Fifth Week of Lent — The Dawn Beyond the Cross _____ 131

Saturday of the Fifth Week of Lent — The Dawn Beyond the Cross _____ 135

The Fifth Sunday of Lent — The Hope That Does Not Disappoint _____ 139

Looking Ahead — Together at the Cross _____ 143

Palm Sunday — The Road That Leads to Love _ 145

Monday in Holy Week — The Fragrance of Love 147

Tuesday in Holy Week — The Grain Falls to the Earth _____ 151

Wednesday in Holy Week — Betrayal in the Night _____ 155

Maundy Thursday — The Basin and the Towel _ 159

Good Friday — The Love That Will Not Let Go __ 163

Holy Saturday — The Silence Between _____ 167

Easter Sunday — The Dawn of All Dawns _____ 171

Sending Forth — The Work of Resurrection ___ 175

Kay Dennis

Benediction	177
Epigraph	xvii
Collect for Lent	xix
Afterword — The Journey Continues	xxi
Blessing for the Road	xxiii
Note on the Scriptures	xxvi
Author's Note	xxix
Acknowledgments	xxxi
About the Author	xxxiii
Other Books by the Author	xxxv
Colophon	xxxvii

From Dust We Walk Together

Kay Dennis

Introduction: Together in Repentance

Lent begins with ashes on our foreheads and a whisper of mortality in our ears: "Remember that you are dust, and to dust you shall return." These words are not meant to shame us; they are meant to bring us home—to remind us that every breath, every act of kindness, every shared sorrow belongs to God. We are dust, yes, but we are dust held together by mercy.

Repentance is often treated as a private matter, a reckoning between one soul and its Maker. Yet Scripture tells a different story. When Nineveh repented, the whole city put on sackcloth. When Israel turned back to God, the people gathered in assembly. Even in the wilderness, Jesus faced temptation not as an isolated mystic but as the one who would bear the weight of a whole community's hunger and hope.

To repent together is to confess that our lives are interwoven—that my healing depends on yours, and yours on mine. It is to look honestly at what separates us from one another and from God, and then to turn, not inward, but toward the Cross where division is undone.

We begin our Lenten pilgrimage side by side. As we kneel, fast, and pray, we do so in communion with saints and sinners alike. In the quiet of shared contrition, we discover that grace does not erase our dust—it gathers it, molds it, and breathes new life into it.

From Dust We Walk Together

May these reflections draw us closer to the Christ who joins us in the ashes and lifts us toward resurrection light.

Ash Wednesday — Marked as One Body

Joel 2:12–17 (NRSV)

Yet even now, says the Lord, return to me with all your heart, with fasting, with weeping, and with mourning; rend your hearts and not your clothing. Return to the Lord, your God, for he is gracious and merciful, slow to anger, and abounding in steadfast love, and relents from punishing. Who knows whether he will not turn and relent, and leave a blessing behind him, a grain offering and a drink offering for the Lord your God?

Blow the trumpet in Zion; sanctify a fast; call a solemn assembly; gather the people. Sanctify the congregation; assemble the aged; gather the children, even infants at the breast. Let the bridegroom leave his room, and the bride her canopy. Between the vestibule and the altar let the priests, the ministers of the Lord, weep. Let them say, 'Spare your people, O Lord, and do not make your heritage a mockery, a byword among the nations. Why should it be said among the peoples, "Where is their God?"'

Reflection

Ash Wednesday calls us back to the beginning—to the first breath that stirred dust into life and to the shared humanity that unites us all. The ashes placed on our foreheads are not private badges of guilt but public signs of belonging. We wear them as one body, marked by grace, shaped by repentance, and dependent upon mercy.

The prophet Joel does not summon individuals in isolation; he calls for a gathering—old and young, married, and single, priest and farmer alike. Lent begins with community. The call is not merely to feel sorrow but to come together before God, naming what is broken among us and within us. When one of us strays, the whole body feels it; when one of us returns, all rejoice.

Our culture prizes independence, but the Gospel invites interdependence. In Christ, no repentance stands alone. Every confession, every tear shed for the world's wounds becomes a thread in the fabric of redemption. To wear ashes is to say: We remember our mortality together—and we trust our resurrection together.

Ash Wednesday is not the end of joy but the beginning of wholeness. The God who calls us to return does not dwell on our failures; He gathers us like dust into His hands and breathes once more the Spirit of life.

Kay Dennis

Prayer

Almighty and everlasting God,
who forgives the sins of all who are penitent:
Create and make in us new and contrite hearts,
that we, worthily lamenting our sins and acknowledging
our wretchedness,
may obtain of you, the God of all mercy, perfect
remission and forgiveness;
through Jesus Christ our Lord. Amen.

Community Practice

Attend an Ash Wednesday service and sit beside someone
you do not know well.
As you receive the ashes, pray silently for that person and
for all who bear the same mark today.
Let the dust on your forehead remind you that repentance
is never solitary—it is the work of the whole Church.

From Dust We Walk Together

Kay Dennis

Thursday after Ash Wednesday — The Dust We Share

Deuteronomy 30:15-20 (NRSV)

See, I have set before you today life and prosperity, death and adversity. If you obey the commandments of the Lord your God that I am commanding you today, by loving the Lord your God, walking in his ways, and observing his commandments, decrees, and ordinances, then you shall live and become numerous, and the Lord your God will bless you in the land that you are entering to possess. But if your heart turns away and you do not hear, but are led astray to bow down to other gods and serve them, I declare to you today that you shall perish; you shall not live long in the land that you are crossing the Jordan to enter and possess. I call heaven and earth to witness against you today that I have set before you life and death, blessings and curses. Choose life so that you and your descendants may live, loving the Lord your God, obeying him, and holding fast to him; for that means life to you and length of days, so that you may live in the land that the Lord swore to give to your ancestors, to Abraham, to Isaac, and to Jacob.

Reflection

The ashes have hardly faded from our brows when Moses' words reach us: "Choose life." Lent, for all its somber tones, is ultimately an invitation into vitality—into the kind of life that can only be found when we turn toward God and one another.

Our choices rarely feel cosmic. They take the form of small daily gestures: to forgive or to hold a grudge, to speak hope or to spread despair, to share bread or to close the door. Yet, Scripture insists these moments matter not just to us, but to the entire body. The covenant of life and blessing is a communal covenant. Heaven and earth are summoned as witnesses because creation itself bends toward our choices.

We are bound together by the dust we share. The same breath of God animates us all. To "choose life" is to choose the flourishing of others—to act and pray in ways that sustain the weakest among us. Every act of mercy is a vote for life; every act of selfishness, a whisper of death. Lent asks us: will the world around us be more alive because of how we live this day?

The path of obedience that Moses describes is not a set of restrictions but a posture of belonging. When we love the Lord our God with all our heart, we learn to love one another with the same fierce tenderness. Dust becomes fertile soil for blessing.

Prayer

Almighty God,
who has given us life and breath and set before us the
way of blessing:
Grant us grace to choose what leads to life,
to walk humbly in Your commandments,
and to seek the good of all whom You have made;
through Jesus Christ our Lord. Amen.

Community Practice

Spend time outdoors today—perhaps walking with a friend or neighbor. Notice how the same wind touches you both. Offer a simple prayer of thanksgiving for the shared breath that sustains all creation and commit to one concrete act that will help another person "choose life" this week.

From Dust We Walk Together

Kay Dennis

Friday after Ash Wednesday — Community of the Penitent

Isaiah 58:1–9a (NRSV)

Shout out, do not hold back! Lift up your voice like a trumpet! Announce to my people their rebellion, to the house of Jacob their sins. Yet day after day they seek me and delight to know my ways, as if they were a nation that practiced righteousness and did not forsake the ordinance of their God; they ask of me righteous judgments, they delight to draw near to God. "Why do we fast, but you do not see? Why humble ourselves, but you do not notice?"

Look, you serve your own interest on your fast day, and oppress all your workers. Look, you fast only to quarrel and to fight and to strike with a wicked fist. Such fasting as you do today will not make your voice heard on high. Is such the fast that I choose, a day to humble oneself? Is it to bow down the head like a bulrush, and to lie in sackcloth and ashes? Will you call this a fast, a day acceptable to the Lord?

Is not this the fast that I choose: to loose the bonds of injustice, to undo the thongs of the yoke, to let the oppressed go free, and to break every yoke? Is it not to share your bread with the hungry, and bring the homeless poor into your house; when you see the naked, to cover them, and not to hide yourself from your own kin? Then your light shall break forth like the dawn, and your healing shall spring up quickly; your vindicator shall go before you; the glory of the Lord shall be your rear guard. Then you shall call, and the Lord will answer; you shall cry for help, and he will say, Here I am.

Reflection

Isaiah's trumpet blast shatters any illusion that repentance can remain internal or theoretical. The prophet's words pierce through our respectable religiosity and reach the hidden places where we separate worship from justice. People who love God must also love their neighbors.

In every generation, the temptation arises to make Lent about appearances: what we give up, what we accomplish, and how disciplined we seem. Yet, God desires not performance but transformation. The fast that pleases the Lord does not end at the altar; it begins there and moves outward—to the streets, the shelters, the strained relationships, and the systems that wound.

True fasting loosens the cords that bind others. It lifts burdens rather than adds them. It shares bread and breaks barriers. When we practice repentance together—each of us acknowledging both personal sin and collective complicity—our light breaks forth, not as individual candles, but as dawn over a landscape once shadowed by indifference.

Isaiah reminds us that the community of the penitent is also the community of the healed. When we stop hiding from our own kin, we discover that forgiveness runs both ways. To confess together is to be restored together.

Prayer

Most merciful Father,
whose prophet taught us that true fasting is justice and compassion:
Deliver us from hollow piety and self-deception,
and give us grace to loose the bonds of the oppressed,
that our light may break forth as the morning;
through Jesus Christ our Lord. Amen.

Community Practice

Choose one local ministry or outreach that serves those in need—shelter, food pantry, prison, or hospital—and offer your time or resources today. Let your fasting from comfort become someone else's feast of hope.

From Dust We Walk Together

Kay Dennis

Saturday after Ash Wednesday — Learning to Kneel Together

Isaiah 58:9b–14 (NRSV)

If you remove the yoke from among you, the pointing of the finger, the speaking of evil, if you offer your food to the hungry and satisfy the needs of the afflicted, then your light shall rise in the darkness and your gloom be like the noonday. The Lord will guide you continually, and satisfy your needs in parched places, and make your bones strong; and you shall be like a watered garden, like a spring of water, whose waters never fail. Your ancient ruins shall be rebuilt; you shall raise up the foundations of many generations; you shall be called the repairer of the breach, the restorer of streets to live in.

If you refrain from trampling the sabbath, from pursuing your own interests on my holy day; if you call the sabbath a delight and the holy day of the Lord honorable; if you honor it, not going your own ways, serving your own interests, or pursuing your own affairs; then you shall take delight in the Lord, and I will make you ride upon the heights of the earth; I will feed you with the heritage of your ancestor Jacob, for the mouth of the Lord has spoken.

Reflection

By the week's end, Isaiah's vision shifts from rebuke to renewal. Having torn down the false walls of piety, God now speaks of rebuilding. "Your ancient ruins shall be rebuilt; you shall be called the repairer of the breach." Repentance is not only confession—it is construction. When we bow down, we make room for new foundations to rise.

Kneeling is not weakness but orientation. To kneel is to recognize where our strength truly lies. When we kneel together, divisions lose their height; pride loses its vantage point. Before the altar, the wealthy, and the poor, the confident and the weary, find themselves side by side—equal dust in the hands of a merciful God. From that humility springs a living hope, one that rebuilds streets, relationships, and even hearts.

The Sabbath imagery here reminds us that restoration requires rhythm. We cannot mend the world on exhaustion. God calls us to rest in Him, to make space for the holy, and to remember that our worth is not measured by production but by presence. Communities that learn to kneel together learn also to rise together.

Prayer

O Lord of mercy and rest,
who rebuilds what pride has ruined and guides Thy
people in parched places:
Teach us to delight in Your Sabbath,
to honor You with humble hearts,
and to rise from our knees as repairers of the breach;
through Jesus Christ our Lord. Amen.

Community Practice

Set aside one hour of quiet today. Turn off devices, silence notifications, and rest. Use that time to pray for someone burdened, and then—if you are able—reach out with an act of kindness or encouragement. Let your rest become part of someone else's rebuilding.

From Dust We Walk Together

Kay Dennis

The First Sunday of Lent — The Wilderness We Don't Face Alone

Matthew 4:1-11 (NRSV)

Then Jesus was led up by the Spirit into the wilderness to be tempted by the devil. He fasted forty days and forty nights, and afterwards he was famished. The tempter came and said to him, "If you are the Son of God, command these stones to become loaves of bread." But he answered, "It is written, 'One does not live by bread alone, but by every word that comes from the mouth of God.'"

Then the devil took him to the holy city and placed him on the pinnacle of the temple, saying to him, "If you are the Son of God, throw yourself down; for it is written, 'He will command his angels concerning you,' and 'On their hands they will bear you up, so that you will not dash your foot against a stone.'" Jesus said to him, "Again it is written, 'Do not put the Lord your God to the test.'"

Again, the devil took him to a very high mountain and showed him all the kingdoms of the world and their splendor; and he said to him, "All these I will give you, if you will fall down and worship me." Jesus said to him, "Away with you, Satan! for it is written, 'Worship the

Lord your God, and serve only him.'" Then the devil left him, and suddenly angels came and waited on him.

Reflection

The wilderness is not an accident in the story of salvation; it is the classroom of faith. Jesus enters its barren silence not as a hermit but as the representative of us all—every hungry, tested soul that has ever wondered where God is when life grows harsh.

Temptation is seldom about obvious evil. More often it is the seduction of easy answers: bread without trust, safety without surrender, glory without love. The devil's offers are shortcuts that bypass community. They whisper, You can do this alone. Yet, Christ refuses isolation. He answers each temptation with the language of belonging—words rooted in Israel's shared memory, in a people who journeyed together through another wilderness.

Our own deserts may look different: grief, addiction, exhaustion, and injustice. But the promise remains—the same Spirit who led Jesus into the wilderness accompanies us still. And just as angels ministered to Him, God sends us companions in unexpected forms: a friend who listens, a congregation that prays, a neighbor who brings soup. Lent is not meant to prove our strength but to reveal God's presence among the weak.

When we face the wilderness together, its desolation becomes a place of communion. There we learn that every hunger is met not by self-sufficiency but by shared dependence on the Word made flesh.

Prayer

Almighty and everlasting God,
whose Son by temptation overcame the tempter:
Grant that we may find strength in His victory,
endure with Him the trials of this life,
and, by Your Spirit, walk together through every wilderness,
through Jesus Christ our Lord. Amen.

Community Practice

Invite someone who seems lonely or burdened to join you for a simple meal this week. Share not solutions but presence. Pray together that both of you may find the Bread that truly satisfies.

From Dust We Walk Together

Kay Dennis

Looking Ahead — Together in Trust

As the first week of Lent closes, we carry the ashes of repentance into the wilderness of faith. The journey ahead will ask not only for humility but for trust—trust that God's mercy endures when the path grows uncertain, and trust that the companions beside us are gifts of grace.

In the coming days, may we learn to walk together in confidence, listening for the quiet voice that leads us from desolation toward delight. For the same Spirit that gathers us in repentance will guide us, side by side, into the fullness of life.

From Dust We Walk Together

Kay Dennis

Monday after the First Sunday of Lent — Nicodemus by Night

John 3:1–17 (NRSV)

Now there was a Pharisee named Nicodemus, a leader of the Jews. He came to Jesus by night and said to him, "Rabbi, we know that you are a teacher who has come from God; for no one can do these signs that you do apart from the presence of God." Jesus answered him, "Very truly, I tell you, no one can see the kingdom of God without being born from above." Nicodemus said to him, "How can anyone be born after having grown old? Can one enter a second time into the mother's womb and be born?" Jesus answered, "Very truly, I tell you, no one can enter the kingdom of God without being born of water and Spirit. What is born of the flesh is flesh, and what is born of the Spirit is spirit."

"Do not be astonished that I said to you, 'You must be born from above.' The wind blows where it chooses, and you hear the sound of it, but you do not know where it comes from or where it goes. So it is with everyone who is born of the Spirit." Nicodemus said to him, "How can these things be?" Jesus answered him, "Are you a teacher of Israel, and yet you do not understand these things?"

"For God so loved the world that he gave his only Son, so that everyone who believes in him may not perish but may have eternal life. Indeed, God did not send the Son into the world to condemn the world, but in order that the world might be saved through him."

Reflection

Nicodemus comes by night, hiding in shadows, searching for something he cannot yet name. His faith is hesitant but real—a flicker of trust that draws him toward the light. The beauty of this story is that Jesus meets him there, in the darkness. Grace does not wait for perfect courage; it begins with a trembling question.

To be "born from above" is not to start over in isolation but to be re-woven into the fabric of divine life. New birth is communal; the Spirit who gives life gathers us into one body. The wind that blows through Nicodemus's confusion is the same breath that fills the Church at Pentecost.

Trust, like birth, is something we rarely manage alone. It is midwifed by others who hold the light when we cannot see. Every congregation has its Nicodemuses—souls who linger at the edge of faith, wondering if they belong. Jesus' nighttime conversation assures us that belonging begins precisely there, where questions outnumber answers.

To believe in Christ is to step from secrecy into fellowship, to discover that eternal life is not merely length of days but depth of relationship: God so loved the world—all of us, together.

Prayer

O God of light and mercy,
who meets us even in our night-time fears:
Grant that we, being born anew of water and the Spirit,
may trust You with open hearts
and walk as children of Your light;
through Jesus Christ our Lord. Amen.

Community Practice

Reach out to someone who has been absent from worship or community life.
Invite them to coffee or simply send a note reminding them they are remembered.
Trust grows in the gentle warmth of being seen and welcomed.

From Dust We Walk Together

Kay Dennis

Tuesday after the First Sunday of Lent — The Tent of Abraham

Genesis 12:1–4a (NRSV)

Now the Lord said to Abram, "Go from your country and your kindred and your father's house to the land that I will show you. I will make of you a great nation, and I will bless you, and make your name great, so that you will be a blessing. I will bless those who bless you, and the one who curses you I will curse; and in you all the families of the earth shall be blessed." So Abram went, as the Lord had told him; and Lot went with him.

Reflection

When Abram heard the voice of God calling him to go, there was no map, no gps, no guarantee, no assurance except the promise that God would be with him. Trust, at its core, is the willingness to move with God even when the destination remains unseen.

Yet, this story is not only about Abram's courage—it is about the community that grew from one act of obedience. God's promise is expansive: "In you all the families of the earth shall be blessed." Abram's faith sets in motion a web of relationships that stretches through generations and nations. His tent becomes a symbol of hospitality, open on all sides, ready to receive strangers who may carry messages of grace.

Trust is seldom a solitary adventure. Even as Abram journeys into the unknown, Lot travels with him; servants and herds follow. The life of faith is lived in company, and every step forward is a communal act of hope. When we walk together—holding one another through fear and fatigue—we embody the very covenant God made with Abram: a people through whom the world will see blessing.

In this Lenten season, we are invited to loosen our grip on certainty and step out under the same vast sky Abram saw. The stars above are reminders that God's promises always outnumber our doubts.

Prayer

O God of our fathers and mothers,
who called Abram to journey toward an unseen land:
Lead us by Your word and Spirit,
that trusting in Your promises,
we may become a blessing to others
and find our home in You,
through Jesus Christ our Lord. Amen.

Kay Dennis

Community Practice

Invite someone to share a meal or conversation who is new to your church, work, or neighborhood.
Practice the hospitality of Abram's tent—open, generous, and expectant of blessing.
Each welcome extended is another step into God's unfolding promise.

From Dust We Walk Together

Kay Dennis

Wednesday after the First Sunday of Lent — Faith Between Friends

Mark 2:1–12 (NRSV)

When he returned to Capernaum after some days, it was reported that he was at home. So many gathered around that there was no longer room for them, not even in front of the door; and he was speaking the word to them. Then some people came, bringing to him a paralyzed man, carried by four of them. And when they could not bring him to Jesus because of the crowd, they removed the roof above him; and after having dug through it, they let down the mat on which the paralytic lay. When Jesus saw their faith, he said to the paralytic, "Son, your sins are forgiven."

Now some of the scribes were sitting there, questioning in their hearts, "Why does this fellow speak in this way? It is blasphemy! Who can forgive sins but God alone?" At once Jesus perceived in his spirit that they were discussing these questions among themselves; and he said to them, "Why do you raise such questions in your hearts? Which is easier, to say to the paralytic, 'Your sins are forgiven,' or to say, 'Stand up and take your mat and walk'? But so that you may know that the Son of Man has authority on earth to forgive sins"—he said to the paralytic—"I say to you, stand up, take your mat and go to your home." And he stood up, and immediately took the mat and went out before all of them; so that they were all amazed and glorified God, saying, "We have never seen anything like this!"

Reflection

The paralyzed man could not reach Jesus on his own. His healing began not with his own faith but with the trust of friends who refused to give up. They lifted him, carried him, tore open a roof, and lowered him into grace. When Jesus "saw their faith," the miracle began.

Faith, it seems, can be borrowed. When one of us falters, another's belief can carry us closer to Christ. Community is not simply a gathering of like-minded people; it is a network of mercy strong enough to bear one another's weight. The Church becomes holy ground whenever we take turns being the ones on the mat and the ones at the corners, holding the ropes.

The scribes who watch from the sidelines cannot see what's happening beneath the dust of falling plaster. They debate theology while love invents its own entrance. In that moment, Jesus reveals that forgiveness and healing are not separate gifts—they are the same restoration, offered to a community that dares to trust together.

Our roofs may look different: pride, decorum, fear of inconvenience. But when compassion tears through such barriers, we glimpse what faith was meant to be—a living bond that makes wholeness possible.

Prayer

Most gracious Lord,
who made us members one of another in Your body:
Give us grace to bear one another's burdens,
to trust You together in weakness and in strength,
and to rejoice when any soul is made whole;
through Jesus Christ our Lord. Amen.

Community Practice

Think of someone whose burdens you can help carry—a friend in crisis, a neighbor in need, a weary caregiver. Offer practical support, prayer, or listening presence. Today, be one of the four who hold the mat.

From Dust We Walk Together

Kay Dennis

Thursday after the First Sunday of Lent — Covenant as Relationship

Romans 4:1–5, 13–17 (NRSV)

What then are we to say was gained by Abraham, our ancestor according to the flesh? For if Abraham was justified by works, he has something to boast about, but not before God. For what does the scripture say? "Abraham believed God, and it was reckoned to him as righteousness." Now to one who works, wages are not reckoned as a gift but as something due. But to one who without works trusts him who justifies the ungodly, such faith is reckoned as righteousness.

For the promise that he would inherit the world did not come to Abraham or to his descendants through the law but through the righteousness of faith. If it is the adherents of the law who are to be the heirs, faith is null and the promise is void. For the law brings wrath; but where there is no law, neither is there violation. For this reason it depends on faith, in order that the promise may rest on grace and be guaranteed to all his descendants, not only to the adherents of the law but also to those who share the faith of Abraham (for he is the father of all of us), as it is written, "I have made you the father of many nations")—in the presence of the God in whom he believed, who gives life to the dead and calls into existence the things that do not exist.

Reflection

Faith, Paul insists, is not a contract—it is a relationship. Abraham's righteousness was not earned; it was given because he trusted the One who gives life to the dead. Covenant, then, is not a legal agreement between equals but the story of a God who keeps reaching out to flawed people, binding them to Himself in love that refuses to quit.

Our modern world prefers transactions: If I do this, I'll get that. But grace cannot be reduced to a formula. It is not the wage for our effort but the gift of belonging. To live by faith is to live in trust of a promise that rests on grace, not performance. The same grace that formed Abraham's faith forms ours—it creates community where none existed, calling into being a people shaped by mercy.

The Church stands as a living sign of that covenant. We are not perfect, but we are bound to one another by a promise larger than our failures. Lent invites us to look again at our relationships—with God, with one another, with the world—and to see them as covenants of care. Where trust has been broken, grace calls us to repair. Where life seems barren, the God who calls things into existence speaks renewal.

Prayer

Faithful God,
who called Abraham from doubt to trust and from barrenness to promise:
Renew in us the covenant of grace,
that, justified not by our merit but by Your mercy,
we may live as a people of faith and friendship;
through Jesus Christ our Lord. Amen.

Community Practice

Write a letter, message, or prayer of reconciliation to someone with whom trust has been strained. Offer it in humility, not to prove yourself right, but to restore the relationship. Covenant faith always begins with grace extended.

From Dust We Walk Together

Kay Dennis

Friday after the First Sunday of Lent — Born of Spirit, Born Together

John 3:5–8 (NRSV)

Jesus answered, "Very truly, I tell you, no one can enter the kingdom of God without being born of water and Spirit. What is born of the flesh is flesh, and what is born of the Spirit is spirit. Do not be astonished that I said to you, 'You must be born from above.' The wind blows where it chooses, and you hear the sound of it, but you do not know where it comes from or where it goes. So it is with everyone who is born of the Spirit."

Reflection

The Spirit, Jesus tells Nicodemus, moves like the wind—free, unpredictable, impossible to control. We cannot trace its origin or dictate its direction, but we can feel its touch, hear its song in the trees, and see its work in changed lives. To be born of the Spirit is to be drawn into this holy movement, carried by grace rather than driven by certainty.

Yet, even in its mystery, the Spirit's work is never solitary. New birth happens in community—within the waters of baptism, the prayers of the faithful, and the lifelong process of becoming who we already are in Christ. The Spirit does not produce spiritual freelancers but forms a body knit together in love. We are born into a family, and the mark of that family is not perfection but presence.

In a culture that prizes autonomy, this can feel uncomfortable. To belong to the Spirit is to relinquish control, to let our boundaries blur into communion. The Spirit reshapes our hearts for hospitality, making room for those whom the world has cast aside. Every time we forgive, welcome, or serve, we participate in this birth that never stops happening.

Lent, then, is not a season of self-improvement but of re-formation—allowing the Spirit to blow through the rooms of our souls and sweep away what no longer gives life. When the wind moves, it gathers; and those born of the Spirit are never alone.

Prayer

Holy Spirit, Breath of God,
who brings life out of dust and unity out of division:
Renew us by Your grace,
that being born anew from above,
we may live as one people in love and truth;
through Jesus Christ our Lord. Amen.

Kay Dennis

Community Practice

Take a moment today to thank someone who has helped nurture your faith—perhaps a teacher, pastor, friend, or family member. Let them know how their presence has been part of your rebirth in the Spirit. Then ask whom you might help nurture in return.

From Dust We Walk Together

Kay Dennis

Saturday after the First Sunday of Lent — Trusting in the Dark

Psalm 121 (NRSV)

> I lift up my eyes to the hills— from where will my help come?
> My help comes from the Lord, who made heaven and earth.
> He will not let your foot be moved; he who keeps you will not slumber.
> He who keeps Israel will neither slumber nor sleep.
> The Lord is your keeper; the Lord is your shade at your right hand.
> The sun shall not strike you by day, nor the moon by night.
> The Lord will keep you from all evil; he will keep your life.
> The Lord will keep your going out and your coming in from this time on and forevermore.

Reflection

Few psalms speak to the heart of trust like this one. These words were likely sung by pilgrims on the road to Jerusalem—ordinary travelers facing uncertain paths, steep climbs, and unseen dangers. Their song begins with a question: "From where will my help come?" and ends with a declaration: "My help comes from the Lord." Faith does not erase fear; it transforms it into prayer.

Trust often grows strongest when visibility is lowest. The psalmist does not promise a smooth journey or an absence of struggle. Instead, he offers a deeper assurance: God's watchful presence endures even when our own vigilance fails. The One who keeps us does not slumber.

In the darkness of doubt, we discover what it means to be a community of pilgrims. None of us see the whole path; each of us carries a fragment of faith to share. When my eyes are too tired to look to the hills, I need you to look for me. When your steps falter, I can lend you my song. Together we become a living psalm, echoing confidence through the valley.

Lent's wilderness can feel long and shadowed, yet this psalm reminds us that trust is not a mood—it is a relationship. The Keeper of Israel keeps us all, holding our going out and our coming in, until dawn breaks on the final hill.

Kay Dennis

Prayer

Eternal Keeper of Israel,
who neither slumbers nor sleeps:
Watch over us in our journeys, guard our hearts in the night,
and teach us to trust Your presence when the path is dark;
through Jesus Christ our Lord. Amen.

Community Practice

Gather a few friends or family members for a short walk or quiet prayer time. As you go, read Psalm 121 aloud together. Notice the world around you—the sky, the trees, the steady rhythm of steps—and let each heartbeat echo the truth: The Lord keeps us still.

From Dust We Walk Together

Kay Dennis

The Second Sunday of Lent — Lifted Eyes, Shared Hope

Romans 4:18–25 (NRSV)

Hoping against hope, he believed that he would become "the father of many nations," according to what was said, "So numerous shall your descendants be." He did not weaken in faith when he considered his own body, which was already as good as dead (for he was about a hundred years old), or when he considered the barrenness of Sarah's womb. No distrust made him waver concerning the promise of God, but he grew strong in his faith as he gave glory to God, being fully convinced that God was able to do what he had promised. Therefore his faith "was reckoned to him as righteousness." Now the words, "it was reckoned to him," were written not for his sake alone, but for ours also. It will be reckoned to us who believe in him who raised Jesus our Lord from the dead, who was handed over to death for our trespasses and was raised for our justification.

Reflection

Abraham's story ends where trust becomes testimony. He had no reason—at least none that the world could see—to keep believing. Every fact argued against him: his age, Sarah's barrenness, the long silence of heaven. And yet he looked up and trusted the promise of the God who gives life to the dead.

"Hope against hope" is not naïve optimism; it is the steady, stubborn confidence that God's mercy outlasts every obstacle. In a community shaped by such trust, despair does not get the final word. We borrow courage from one another; when one person's faith flickers, another's burns a little brighter to light the way. Together we discover that the promise spoken to Abraham is spoken to us as well: life will spring up where none was expected.

Paul tells us that this ancient faith is not a relic but a living inheritance. Each generation must decide whether to trust the same God who raised Jesus from the dead. Every time we gather at the Table or speak the Creed, we proclaim again that the impossible has already happened. Resurrection has entered the story; therefore, we may trust even in the dark.

To lift our eyes in Lent is not to escape the wilderness but to see beyond it—to glimpse the horizon of a kingdom being born among us, one act of shared hope at a time.

Prayer

Almighty God,
who strengthened Abraham's faith when all seemed lost:
Increase in us the grace of hope,
that, trusting in Your power to raise the dead,
we may glorify You in every trial
and rejoice together in Your promises;
through Jesus Christ our Lord. Amen.

Community Practice

Spend a few minutes today writing down one promise of God that feels hard to believe right now. Share it with a trusted friend or small group and ask them to hold it in prayer with you this week. Hope becomes stronger when it is shared.

From Dust We Walk Together

Kay Dennis

Monday of the Third Week of Lent — The Well at Noon

John 4:5–15 (NRSV)

So he came to a Samaritan city called Sychar, near the plot of ground that Jacob had given to his son Joseph. Jacob's well was there, and Jesus, tired out by his journey, was sitting by the well. It was about noon. A Samaritan woman came to draw water, and Jesus said to her, "Give me a drink." (His disciples had gone to the city to buy food.) The Samaritan woman said to him, "How is it that you, a Jew, ask a drink of me, a woman of Samaria?" (Jews do not share things in common with Samaritans.) Jesus answered her, "If you knew the gift of God, and who it is that is saying to you, 'Give me a drink,' you would have asked him, and he would have given you living water." The woman said to him, "Sir, you have no bucket, and the well is deep. Where do you get that living water? Are you greater than our ancestor Jacob, who gave us the well, and with his sons and his flocks drank from it?" Jesus said to her, "Everyone who drinks of this water will be thirsty again, but those who drink of the water that I will give them will never be thirsty. The water that I will give will become in them a spring of water gushing up to eternal life." The woman said to him, "Sir, give me this water, so that I may never be thirsty or have to keep coming here to draw water."

Reflection

It is noon—the hour when the sun shows no mercy. Most villagers draw their water in the cool of morning, but this woman comes when the streets are empty. She carries more than a jar; she carries the weight of isolation, of whispered stories and half-remembered shame. And there, at the hottest hour, Jesus waits.

The conversation that follows is not about water only. It is about being seen and not condemned, known, and still loved. The one who asks for a drink is the same who offers living water—an exchange that turns scarcity into abundance. The miracle begins not with revelation but with relationship: a Jewish man and a Samaritan woman daring to speak across centuries of prejudice.

We, too, come to the well at odd hours, when thirst and fatigue finally silence our defenses. And Jesus meets us there—unhurried, unashamed to ask for our help before offering His own. He dignifies human need, showing that salvation is not an escape from thirst but a transformation of it. When His living water begins to flow, it does not pool around one soul; it spills outward, quenching an entire community.

The woman who once hid in the heat becomes the first evangelist of her town. The well that marked her shame becomes the fountain of her witness. That is how grace works: what once isolated us becomes the meeting place of redemption.

Prayer

O Christ, Fountain of living water,
who met the Samaritan woman in the heat of day:
Quench the thirst of our hearts,
wash away the dust of fear and division,
and make of Your Church a well of welcome for all;
through Jesus Christ our Lord. Amen.

Community Practice

Share a cup of coffee, tea, or water with someone outside your usual circle—a neighbor, coworker, or stranger. Listen more than you speak. Let the conversation itself become a well where grace can rise.

From Dust We Walk Together

Kay Dennis

Tuesday of the Third Week of Lent — Thirst for Understanding

John 4:27–42 (NRSV)

Just then his disciples came. They were astonished that he was speaking with a woman, but no one said, "What do you want?" or, "Why are you speaking with her?" Then the woman left her water jar and went back to the city. She said to the people, "Come and see a man who told me everything I have ever done! He cannot be the Messiah, can he?" They left the city and were on their way to him.

Meanwhile the disciples were urging him, "Rabbi, eat something." But he said to them, "I have food to eat that you do not know about." So the disciples said to one another, "Surely no one has brought him something to eat?" Jesus said to them, "My food is to do the will of him who sent me and to complete his work. Do you not say, 'Four months more, then comes the harvest'? But I tell you, look around you, and see how the fields are ripe for harvesting."

Many Samaritans from that city believed in him because of the woman's testimony, "He told me everything I have ever done." So when the Samaritans came to him, they asked him to stay with them; and he stayed there two days. And many more believed because of his word. They said to the woman, "It is no longer because of what you said that we believe, for we have heard for ourselves, and we know that this is truly the Savior of the world."

Reflection

The woman leaves her water jar behind—a silent, eloquent detail. The symbol of her daily labor, her isolation, and her thirst is forgotten at the feet of Christ. Something within her has shifted. The one who avoided the crowd now becomes its herald: "Come and see!"

The disciples return from the marketplace with food and find their Teacher filled in a way they cannot understand. They, too, must learn what the woman has just discovered—that God's nourishment is found in relationship, not transaction. The living water and the hidden food are the same gift: communion with the divine love that crosses boundaries and gathers strangers into family.

This story overflows with reversals. The teacher becomes the student. The outcast becomes the evangelist. The "foreigners" become the first to recognize Jesus as the Savior of the world. Understanding in God's kingdom is not reserved for the learned but given to those whose hearts are open.

When the Samaritans invite Jesus to stay, He abides with them for two days—two days of shared meals, shared stories, shared grace. In that time, thirst becomes fellowship. The well of understanding is dug not by argument but by presence.

Lent teaches us that when we drop the jars of self-defense and pretense, we, too, become vessels of living water. The miracle begins when we stop guarding our wells and start inviting others to draw.

Prayer

Lord Jesus Christ,
who satisfies the thirst of all who seek You in truth:
Teach us to lay aside the jars of pride and fear,
that drinking deeply of Your mercy,
we may bring others to the fountain of life;
who livest and reignest with the Father and the Holy Spirit, one God, now and for ever. Amen.

Community Practice

Invite someone into conversation who sees faith differently than you do. Listen with curiosity, not judgment. Let mutual respect be the bucket that draws understanding from the deep well of God's truth.

From Dust We Walk Together

Kay Dennis

Wednesday of the Third Week of Lent — When Thirst Becomes Prayer

Exodus 17:1–7 (NRSV)

From the wilderness of Sin the whole congregation of the Israelites journeyed by stages, as the Lord commanded. They camped at Rephidim, but there was no water for the people to drink. The people quarreled with Moses, and said, "Give us water to drink." Moses said to them, "Why do you quarrel with me? Why do you test the Lord?" But the people thirsted there for water; and the people complained against Moses and said, "Why did you bring us out of Egypt, to kill us and our children and livestock with thirst?"

So Moses cried out to the Lord, "What shall I do with this people? They are almost ready to stone me." The Lord said to Moses, "Go on ahead of the people, and take some of the elders of Israel with you; take in your hand the staff with which you struck the Nile, and go. I will be standing there in front of you on the rock at Horeb. Strike the rock, and water will come out of it, so that the people may drink." Moses did so, in the sight of the elders of Israel. He called the place Massah and Meribah, because the Israelites quarreled and tested the Lord, saying, "Is the Lord among us or not?"

Reflection

In the desert, thirst becomes desperation. The people's cries are not polite prayers—they are the raw language of survival. They do not simply ask for water; they demand it. Yet even in their grumbling, God listens. The miracle of Rephidim is not only that water flows from a rock, but that divine mercy flows toward a complaining people.

We might imagine that faith forbids frustration, but Scripture tells a different story. God can handle our anger, our confusion, our questions. Honest thirst, even when expressed as complaint, can be a form of prayer. The real danger lies not in shouting at God, but in giving up speaking to God altogether.

Notice that God's answer involves the community: Moses must bring the elders; the people must gather to witness. The provision comes not in isolation but in assembly. When the water gushes forth, everyone drinks—the faithful and the fearful alike. Grace is never rationed.

Lent invites us to name our thirsts before God—the thirst for meaning, justice, forgiveness, peace—and to believe that God still stands before the rock. Sometimes our hardest prayers sound more like protests than hymns, but both are heard by the same listening Love.

Prayer

O God, our Rock and our Redeemer,
who brings forth water from the hard stone:
Hear the cries of Your people in every wilderness.
Quench our thirst with the living streams of Your mercy,
that we may trust You even when the springs seem dry;
through Jesus Christ our Lord. Amen.

Community Practice

Today, pray aloud for someone whose voice goes unheard—a neighbor in need, a marginalized community, or a person suffering silently. Let their thirst join yours as a single prayer before God and believe that mercy will flow for all.

From Dust We Walk Together

Kay Dennis

Thursday of the Third Week of Lent — The Song of the Parched

Psalm 63:1–8 (NRSV)

> O God, you are my God, I seek you,
> my soul thirsts for you; my flesh faints for you,
> as in a dry and weary land where there is no water.
> So I have looked upon you in the sanctuary,
> beholding your power and glory.
> Because your steadfast love is better than life,
> my lips will praise you.
> So I will bless you as long as I live;
> I will lift up my hands and call on your name.
> My soul is satisfied as with a rich feast,
> and my mouth praises you with joyful lips
> when I think of you on my bed,
> and meditate on you in the watches of the night;
> for you have been my help,
> and in the shadow of your wings I sing for joy.
> My soul clings to you;
> your right hand upholds me.

Reflection

This psalm was likely composed in the wilderness, far from temple walls, yet its tone is not despair—it is adoration. The writer thirsts not only for water but for God Himself. And in that yearning, worship is born. The song of the parched is one of the most profound acts of faith: to bless God not because life is full, but because God is present even when life feels empty.

When we are spiritually dry, our prayers may come out cracked and uneven, like the desert floor. But in the dryness, something miraculous can happen. Thirst clarifies desire; it reveals what truly sustains us. The psalmist discovers that God's steadfast love is better than life. That realization transforms absence into intimacy—distance into devotion.

In community, this song becomes our shared heartbeat. When one voice falters, another continues. The congregation becomes a choir of longing and gratitude, echoing across generations. Each note of praise, however faint, joins the melody of those who have sung from exile, from prison, from hospital rooms and lonely nights. Together, we learn that praise is not a luxury but a lifeline.

Kay Dennis

Prayer

O Lord, our Desire and our Delight,
whose love is better than life itself:
Satisfy our souls in dry places,
teach our lips to praise You in the night,
and uphold us beneath the shadow of Your wings;
through Jesus Christ our Lord. Amen.

Community Practice

Read Psalm 63 aloud, either alone or with a small group. As you speak the words, pause after each verse that stirs your heart. Let the silences become part of the prayer. Thirst, too, has a sound when it is offered to God.

From Dust We Walk Together

Kay Dennis

Friday of the Third Week of Lent — The Table in the Desert

Isaiah 55:1–3 (NRSV)

> Ho, everyone who thirsts, come to the waters;
> and you that have no money, come, buy and eat!
> Come, buy wine and milk without money and without price.
> Why do you spend your money for that which is not bread,
> and your labor for that which does not satisfy?
> Listen carefully to me, and eat what is good,
> and delight yourselves in rich food.
> Incline your ear, and come to me;
> listen, so that you may live.
> I will make with you an everlasting covenant,
> my steadfast, sure love for David.

Reflection

The prophet's cry echoes like a trumpet across the wilderness: "Come, everyone who thirsts!" It is not a command but an invitation—urgent, inclusive, overflowing with grace. Isaiah imagines a banquet where the hungry are fed, the poor are honored, and the weary are welcomed without cost. God's table is set not in the palace but in the desert.

Every human heart spends itself on things that cannot satisfy—success, control, recognition, possessions—and still we thirst. Lent exposes the emptiness of such pursuits and reawakens our appetite for what truly nourishes. The divine invitation is startling in its generosity: "Come, buy without money." The economy of grace cannot be earned or hoarded; it must be received and shared.

Notice how the prophet links hearing and eating: "Listen carefully to me, and eat what is good." The feast begins with attention. When we listen for the Word, we begin to taste life's true sweetness. This is the nourishment that builds community—bread that strengthens, wine that gladdens, milk that sustains. At this table, we learn again that abundance is not measured by what we own, but by whom we include.

Prayer

Bountiful Lord,
who invites the thirsty to Your table without price:
Open our ears to Your Word and our hearts to Your feast,
that feeding on Your mercy,
we may share Your abundance with all who hunger;
through Jesus Christ our Lord. Amen.

Community Practice

Prepare a simple meal and invite others to join you—especially someone who might be alone. Keep it unpretentious: bread, soup, water, laughter. Let the table itself become a sacrament of grace freely given and joy freely shared.

From Dust We Walk Together

Kay Dennis

Saturday of the Third Week of Lent — The Well Revisited

John 7:37–39 (NRSV)

On the last day of the festival, the great day, while Jesus was standing there, he cried out, "Let anyone who is thirsty come to me, and let the one who believes in me drink. As the scripture has said, 'Out of the believer's heart shall flow rivers of living water.'" Now he said this about the Spirit, which believers in him were to receive; for as yet there was no Spirit, because Jesus was not yet glorified.

Reflection

The story of the well comes full circle here. Earlier, Jesus offered living water to one woman in the heat of the day; now, He offers it publicly to all who thirst. What began as a private encounter has become a universal invitation. The water is not meant to be stored—it is meant to flow.

Notice how the promise expands: those who drink of Christ's Spirit will themselves become fountains. Grace received becomes grace released. The believer's heart is transformed into a riverbed through which God's life moves into the world. In a culture obsessed with scarcity, this vision of abundance is radical. It declares that the Spirit's generosity is not a limited resource; the more it flows, the stronger it becomes.

Lent reminds us that the Church is meant to be a well, not a reservoir. When communities cling to their blessings instead of sharing them, the water stagnates. But when love pours outward—through forgiveness, justice, hospitality—the desert blooms again.

Perhaps that is why Jesus cried out in public, voice lifted above the noise of the festival. He wanted the whole crowd to hear that their deepest thirst could only be met in Him—and that once it was, they would never be the same.

Prayer

Living Christ,
Fountain of all mercy and Source of every blessing:
Fill us with Your Spirit,
that out of the dryness of our hearts may flow rivers of compassion and joy,
bringing life wherever we go;
who lives and reigns with the Father and the Holy Spirit,
one God, now and for ever. Amen.

Kay Dennis

Community Practice

Bring a small gift of refreshment to someone this weekend—a bottle of water for a worker outdoors, a meal for a neighbor, a note of encouragement for a friend. Let a simple act of kindness become a stream of living water flowing through your day.

From Dust We Walk Together

Kay Dennis

The Third Sunday of Lent — Streams in the Desert

Isaiah 35:1–7 (NRSV)

> The wilderness and the dry land shall be glad,
> the desert shall rejoice and blossom;
> like the crocus it shall blossom abundantly,
> and rejoice with joy and singing.
> The glory of Lebanon shall be given to it,
> the majesty of Carmel and Sharon.
> They shall see the glory of the Lord,
> the majesty of our God.
>
> Strengthen the weak hands,
> and make firm the feeble knees.
> Say to those who are of a fearful heart,
> "Be strong, do not fear!
> Here is your God.
> He will come with vengeance,
> with terrible recompense.
> He will come and save you."
>
> Then the eyes of the blind shall be opened,
> and the ears of the deaf unstopped;
> then the lame shall leap like a deer,

and the tongue of the speechless sing for joy.
For waters shall break forth in the wilderness,
and streams in the desert;
the burning sand shall become a pool,
and the thirsty ground springs of water.

Reflection

Isaiah's vision is an eruption of joy in a landscape of desolation. The wilderness that once swallowed travelers now sings. The parched earth bursts into bloom; dry riverbeds become fountains. It is a picture of God's redemption written in the language of creation itself.

We often imagine salvation as escape—from trouble, from pain, from the desert. But Isaiah reminds us that God's salvation transforms rather than abandons. The same wilderness that once drained us becomes the place of our renewal. The people who have walked in fear are now told to strengthen one another's hands and hearts. Redemption begins when community itself becomes an oasis.

Notice that this miracle is communal. The weak need encouragers; the fearful need companions. The blind and the lame are lifted not only by God's power but by the shared joy of those who have seen the streams begin to flow. The new creation Isaiah imagines is not solitary bliss but collective flourishing. It is the fulfillment of every

Lenten longing—the dry places of our souls flowering under grace.

When the desert sings, it sings in harmony. Its streams do not belong to any one pilgrim; they belong to all who thirst. That is the promise of Lent: even in the wilderness, there is water enough for everyone.

Prayer

Creator and Redeemer,
who makes the desert rejoice and the barren land to bloom:
Pour upon us Your living water,
that our dry hearts may blossom with compassion and hope,
and that our lives may refresh all who journey beside us;
through Jesus Christ our Lord. Amen.

Community Practice

Find one concrete way to bring refreshment to your community this week—perhaps planting flowers in a neglected space, writing a note of encouragement, or organizing a small act of kindness. Even a single drop of grace can help a desert bloom.

From Dust We Walk Together

Kay Dennis

Looking Ahead — Together in Light

The wells have been filled, the streams have begun to flow, and the thirsty ground is singing again. We have learned that thirst is not our enemy—it is our teacher. It draws us toward God and toward one another. We have watched the Samaritan woman drop her jar, Moses strike the rock, and Isaiah's desert blossom. In each story, longing became invitation, and emptiness became abundance.

But the journey continues. Lent does not end with refreshment; it moves toward revelation. The One who gives water will soon open our eyes to the deeper miracle: light shining in the darkness, truth piercing through denial, and mercy illuminating all that once hid in shadow.

To walk together in light is to see each other clearly—to behold the divine image even in the faces we struggle to understand. It is to let illumination become vocation, carrying the glow of grace into the corners of our communities. The wells of thirst have become lamps of faith.

As we step into the next week, may we walk as children of the day, trusting that every drop of living water we have received will reflect the radiance of the One who is both Light and Life.

From Dust We Walk Together

Kay Dennis

Monday of the Fourth Week of Lent — Eyes Opened at Emmaus

Luke 24:13–32 (NRSV)

Now on that same day two of them were going to a village called Emmaus, about seven miles from Jerusalem, and talking with each other about all these things that had happened. While they were talking and discussing, Jesus himself came near and went with them, but their eyes were kept from recognizing him.

And he said to them, "What are you discussing with each other while you walk along?" They stood still, looking sad. Then one of them, whose name was Cleopas, answered him, "Are you the only stranger in Jerusalem who does not know the things that have taken place there in these days?" He asked them, "What things?" They replied, "The things about Jesus of Nazareth, who was a prophet mighty in deed and word before God and all the people, and how our chief priests and leaders handed him over to be condemned to death and crucified him. But we had hoped that he was the one to redeem Israel."

Then he said to them, "Oh, how foolish you are, and how slow of heart to believe all that the prophets have declared! Was it not necessary that the Messiah should suffer these things and then enter into his glory?" Then beginning with Moses and all the prophets, he interpreted to them the things about himself in all the scriptures. As they came near the village to which they were going, he walked ahead as if he were going on. But they urged him strongly, saying, "Stay with us, because it is almost evening and the day is now nearly over." So he went in to stay with them. When he was at the table with them, he took bread, blessed and broke it, and gave it to them. Then their eyes were opened, and they recognized him; and he vanished from their sight. They said to each other, "Were not our hearts burning within us while he was talking to us on the road, while he was opening the scriptures to us?"

Reflection

The road to Emmaus is the road of disappointment. Two disciples walk away from Jerusalem carrying the weight of shattered hopes: "We had hoped he was the one." Their grief blinds them to the very presence of the risen Christ beside them. Yet Jesus does not rebuke their sadness; He joins it. He walks with them, listens to them, and gently re-teaches the story of salvation until their confusion begins to glow with meaning.

This is how divine light often comes—not in flashes of revelation, but in the slow warmth of companionship. The risen Christ is revealed not through spectacle but through Scripture and the simple act of breaking bread. Recognition happens in relationship.

Kay Dennis

The disciples' invitation—"Stay with us, for it is evening"—becomes a prayer for us all. When the road grows long and the day dim, we discover light by holding one another in conversation, by opening our hearts to the stranger who might just be Christ in disguise. Lent's promise of illumination is not an escape from sorrow, but its transformation into communion.

Prayer

Lord Jesus, Light of the world,
who walks beside Your bewildered disciples:
Kindle in our hearts the fire of understanding,
open our eyes to Your presence in the breaking of bread,
and grant that our journey may lead always toward You.
who livest and reignest with the Father and the Holy
Spirit, one God, now and for ever. Amen.

Community Practice

Share a meal this week with someone who is grieving or doubting. You need not offer explanations—only presence. Break bread together and trust that Christ walks unseen between you.

From Dust We Walk Together

Kay Dennis

Tuesday of the Fourth Week of Lent — Light for the Blind

John 9:1–11 (NRSV)

As he walked along, he saw a man blind from birth. His disciples asked him, "Rabbi, who sinned, this man or his parents, that he was born blind?" Jesus answered, "Neither this man nor his parents sinned; he was born blind so that God's works might be revealed in him. We must work the works of him who sent me while it is day; night is coming when no one can work. As long as I am in the world, I am the light of the world." When he had said this, he spat on the ground and made mud with the saliva and spread the mud on the man's eyes, saying to him, "Go, wash in the pool of Siloam" (which means Sent). Then he went and washed and came back able to see. The neighbors and those who had seen him before as a beggar began to ask, "Is this not the man who used to sit and beg?" Some were saying, "It is he." Others were saying, "No, but it is someone like him." He kept saying, "I am the man." But they kept asking him, "Then how were your eyes opened?" He answered, "The man called Jesus made mud, spread it on my eyes, and said to me, 'Go to Siloam and wash.' Then I went and washed and received my sight."

Reflection

Light often begins with touch. Before the blind man can see, he feels the cool earth pressed gently over his eyes—the same dust from which humanity was formed. Jesus' healing is intimate and earthy. He does not stand at a distance commanding sight; He stoops down into the clay, mixing divine breath with soil. Creation begins again.

The disciples' question—"Who sinned?"—is the question of every age. We still look for someone to blame when suffering enters the picture. But Jesus refuses to participate in the calculus of guilt. The blindness is not punishment; it is a stage upon which God's mercy can shine. Every human frailty becomes, in His hands, an opportunity for revelation.

When the man returns from Siloam able to see, he becomes a witness to more than physical sight. He has encountered the Light of the world, and that light will expose the spiritual blindness of those who cannot rejoice in his healing. True vision always unsettles comfortable darkness.

Lent calls us to that same pool of washing, where we allow Christ's touch to remake our sight—to see others not as problems to explain but as lives through whom God's glory might yet be revealed. When we look at one another with eyes formed by mercy, the world itself grows brighter.

Kay Dennis

Prayer

O Christ, Light of the world,
who opens the eyes of the blind and the hearts of the doubting:
Anoint us with Your healing touch,
that seeing others through Your mercy,
we may become bearers of light to all who walk in darkness;
through Jesus Christ our Lord. Amen.

Community Practice

Spend a day paying attention to the "unseen" people around you—workers, caretakers, or neighbors often overlooked. Acknowledge them with kindness, a word, or a smile. Illumination begins in recognition.

From Dust We Walk Together

Kay Dennis

Wednesday of the Fourth Week of Lent — Carried into the Light

Mark 2:1–5 (NRSV)

When he returned to Capernaum after some days, it was reported that he was at home. So many gathered around that there was no longer room for them, not even in front of the door; and he was speaking the word to them. Then some people came, bringing to him a paralyzed man, carried by four of them. And when they could not bring him to Jesus because of the crowd, they removed the roof above him; and after having dug through it, they let down the mat on which the paralytic lay. When Jesus saw their faith, he said to the paralytic, "Son, your sins are forgiven."

Reflection

The man on the mat could not reach the Light on his own. His healing began with the faith of friends who refused to let the crowd or the roof stand in their way. They carried him—literally—into grace. When Jesus "saw their faith," He responded with forgiveness and restoration.

So often we imagine faith as an individual possession, but this story shows its truer form: a shared lifeline. There are days when one soul cannot believe enough to move; on those days, the community carries the mat. Faith becomes tangible in compassion.

The light that floods this scene is not only the glow of physical healing but the radiance of communal love. Roof tiles scatter, sunlight spills into the room, and in that brightness, both body and soul are made whole. The friends' determination breaks through every barrier, teaching us that love's persistence is its own kind of revelation.

Lent reminds us that none of us makes the journey alone. To be part of Christ's body is to take turns being the one lifted and the one lifting, the one forgiven and the one who intercedes. The roof of isolation comes off when we love one another enough to risk interruption.

Prayer

O Merciful Savior,
whose word brings light and whose love restores the broken:
Give us courage to carry one another into Your presence,
and grant that our compassion may open roofs of resistance
until every soul may see Your healing light;

through Jesus Christ our Lord. Amen.

Community Practice

Think of someone in your circle who feels "stuck"—by illness, fear, grief, or loneliness. Gather a few others to pray for and encourage that person. A phone call, meal, or simple note can become the rope that lowers them gently into grace.

From Dust We Walk Together

Kay Dennis

Thursday of the Fourth Week of Lent — Light in Unexpected Places

John 8:12–20 (NRSV)

Again Jesus spoke to them, saying, "I am the light of the world. Whoever follows me will never walk in darkness but will have the light of life." Then the Pharisees said to him, "You are testifying on your own behalf; your testimony is not valid." Jesus answered, "Even if I testify on my own behalf, my testimony is valid because I know where I have come from and where I am going, but you do not know where I come from or where I am going. You judge by human standards; I judge no one. Yet even if I do judge, my judgment is valid; for it is not I alone who judge, but I and the Father who sent me. In your law it is written that the testimony of two witnesses is valid. I testify on my own behalf, and the Father who sent me testifies on my behalf." Then they said to him, "Where is your Father?" Jesus answered, "You know neither me nor my Father. If you knew me, you would know my Father also." He spoke these words while he was teaching in the treasury of the temple, but no one arrested him, because his hour had not yet come.

Reflection

The treasury of the temple was not the obvious place for revelation. It was a busy, noisy court where pilgrims exchanged coins and priests collected offerings. Yet it is there—in the midst of commerce and distraction—that Jesus proclaims, "I am the light of the world." The setting itself is part of the message: divine light shines not in sanctuaries alone, but in the everyday spaces where human life hums and collides.

Those who question Him cannot see what is before them. They are too bound by rules of evidence, too sure that truth must fit their logic. But light does not argue—it reveals. It exposes both the dust on the floor and the gold in the corner. It teaches us to see as God sees, without fear of what will be uncovered.

For Jesus, to walk in the light is not to escape the world's chaos but to navigate it faithfully, guided by the Father's presence. The Pharisees ask, "Where is your Father?" They cannot yet perceive that the Father is standing beside them, incarnate in the Son.

Lent draws us toward this same illumination: the realization that God's presence often hides in plain sight—in conversations at the market, in laughter over coffee, in the quiet persistence of love. The light of Christ still appears in unexpected places, waiting for hearts open enough to notice.

Kay Dennis

Prayer

O Light of the world,
who shinest in places both sacred and ordinary:
Dispel the shadows of our certainty,
that we may behold Thy glory in the faces and moments we overlook,
and walk in the brightness of Thy truth;
through Jesus Christ our Lord. Amen.

Community Practice

Spend part of your day in an ordinary place—a coffee shop, grocery store, or park—and intentionally look for glimpses of God's light. A kind exchange, a moment of laughter, or an act of patience may be the temple treasury where Christ is teaching still.

From Dust We Walk Together

Kay Dennis

Friday of the Fourth Week of Lent — When the Light Exposes Us

John 8:1–11 (NRSV)

Early in the morning he came again to the temple. All the people came to him and he sat down and began to teach them. The scribes and the Pharisees brought a woman who had been caught in adultery; and making her stand before all of them, they said to him, "Teacher, this woman was caught in the very act of committing adultery. Now in the law Moses commanded us to stone such women. Now what do you say?" They said this to test him, so that they might have some charge to bring against him. Jesus bent down and wrote with his finger on the ground. When they kept on questioning him, he straightened up and said to them, "Let anyone among you who is without sin be the first to throw a stone at her." And once again he bent down and wrote on the ground. When they heard it, they went away, one by one, beginning with the elders; and Jesus was left alone with the woman standing before him. Jesus straightened up and said to her, "Woman, where are they? Has no one condemned you?" She said, "No one, sir." And Jesus said, "Neither do I condemn you. Go your way, and from now on do not sin again."

Reflection

There is a moment in every life when the light feels too bright—when our flaws, failures, or secrets are laid bare before others or before God. The woman in this story knows that moment all too well. Dragged into public humiliation, she stands in the center of a circle of accusation. Yet instead of judgment, she encounters mercy.

Jesus' response is not to argue with the law or deny her sin; He simply bends down and writes in the dust. The ground becomes His page, the dust His ink—perhaps to remind those watching that all of them are made of the same fragile earth. When He stands and speaks, His words shift the balance entirely: "Let anyone among you who is without sin be the first to throw a stone." The crowd disperses. Condemnation gives way to compassion. The light has exposed everyone equally, and in that exposure, healing begins.

This is the paradox of divine light—it reveals not to shame but to save. When we allow God to uncover the hidden corners of our hearts, we discover that grace has already arrived there first. Lent invites us to such holy exposure, to stand before the Light that sees everything and still says, "Neither do I condemn you."

Kay Dennis

Prayer

Merciful Lord,
whose light reveals our sin yet refuses our shame:
Shine upon us with the radiance of Your forgiveness,
that standing in Your truth,
we may walk henceforth in freedom and grace;
through Jesus Christ our Lord. Amen.

Community Practice

Reflect on an area of your life where you have felt judged or have judged others. Pray for the humility to see yourself and others as Christ sees you—through eyes of truth and compassion. Then perform one act of kindness that replaces condemnation with mercy.

From Dust We Walk Together

Kay Dennis

Saturday of the Fourth Week of Lent — Reflections of the Light

Matthew 5:14–16 (NRSV)

"You are the light of the world. A city built on a hill cannot be hidden. No one after lighting a lamp puts it under the bushel basket, but on the lampstand, and it gives light to all in the house. In the same way, let your light shine before others, so that they may see your good works and give glory to your Father in heaven."

Reflection

After days of hearing Jesus proclaim "I am the light of the world," we suddenly hear Him say to us, "You are the light of the world." The shift is astonishing. The divine radiance that once seemed so distant is now entrusted to human hands and hearts. Lent's purpose is not only to draw us toward the light but to make us its reflection.

Jesus does not say, "You will become the light," as though it were an achievement, but "You are." The lamp has already been lit; the question is whether we will hide it or let it shine. Light is meant for generosity, not display.

Its calling is to illuminate, not to impress. When we live with compassion, integrity, and hope, we participate in God's illumination of the world.

This light is not ours alone. It is communal, a constellation of small flames that together form the Church's witness. A single candle may flicker, but a city of lamps cannot be hidden. In community, our light grows stronger, brighter, steadier.

To let our light shine is not arrogance—it is obedience. It is the quiet confidence that the same God who spoke "Let there be light" at creation continues to speak through us, kindling faith in others. Every act of mercy, every word of encouragement, every gesture of peace becomes a reflection of divine brilliance in a darkened world.

Prayer

Radiant Lord,
who has kindled in us the light of Your Spirit:
Grant that our lives may shine with compassion and truth,
that in seeing our good works,
others may give glory to You,
the Source and Giver of all light;
through Jesus Christ our Lord. Amen.

Kay Dennis

Community Practice

Light a candle this evening and place it in a window. As it burns, pray for your community—that every home, church, and heart may become a beacon of grace. Let its glow remind you that even the smallest flame can pierce the deepest night.

From Dust We Walk Together

Kay Dennis

The Fourth Sunday of Lent — Walking as Children of the Light

Ephesians 5:8–14 (NRSV)

For once you were darkness, but now in the Lord you are light. Live as children of light—for the fruit of the light is found in all that is good and right and true. Try to find out what is pleasing to the Lord. Take no part in the unfruitful works of darkness, but instead expose them. For it is shameful even to mention what such people do secretly; but everything exposed by the light becomes visible, for everything that becomes visible is light. Therefore it says, "Sleeper, awake! Rise from the dead, and Christ will shine on you."

Reflection

Paul's words do not merely describe a moral transformation—they proclaim an identity. "You are light." Not merely in the light, not just guided by it—you are it. The gospel's brilliance does not simply shine upon believers; it shines through them.

Yet this light is not self-made. It is a gift, born of grace and sustained by the Spirit. Paul reminds the early

Church that they once lived in darkness—caught in patterns of fear, greed, and self-interest—but Christ's radiance has awakened them. To live as children of light is to reflect that awakening in daily choices: goodness instead of bitterness, truth instead of pretense, courage instead of complicity.

When the light of Christ exposes what is hidden, its purpose is not humiliation but healing. The same beam that reveals our faults also reveals the path toward wholeness. In this way, Lent is both mirror and lantern—it shows us who we are and guides us toward who we can become.

The hymn Paul quotes, "Sleeper, awake!" still calls across centuries. It is a resurrection cry, a summons to rise from whatever tombs of complacency or despair hold us. And when we rise, we rise together. A single candle gives warmth; a community of lights transforms the night.

Prayer

Christ our Light,
who awakens those who sleep and illumines those who seek:
Shine upon us, that we may walk as children of the day,
bearing the fruit of all that is good, right, and true;
and kindle in us the courage to be Thy light in the world;
through Jesus Christ our Lord. Amen.

Kay Dennis

Community Practice

Spend time reflecting on what "walking as a child of the light" means in your context—your neighborhood, workplace, or congregation. Identify one specific way you can bring clarity, compassion, or justice to a shadowed place this week, and act on it.

From Dust We Walk Together

Kay Dennis

Looking Ahead — Together in Hope

The light has revealed much.

We have walked beside the risen Christ on the Emmaus Road, watched blind eyes open, roofs broken, and lives restored. We have seen how divine illumination exposes not only what is wrong but what is possible—how mercy transforms judgment, and how a single flame kindled in love can brighten the shadows of an entire community.

Yet Lent is not only a season of seeing; it is a season of becoming. The light now turns toward its deepest mystery—the hope that emerges not from success or certainty, but from the cross itself. Soon we will enter the long shadows of Holy Week, where the brightness of God's love will meet the darkness of human despair. There, hope will be tested and transfigured.

To walk together in hope is not to deny suffering; it is to trust that even suffering can be redeemed. Hope is the steady flame that refuses to die, the quiet assurance that the story is not over, that dawn still waits beyond the hill. We go forward now as bearers of that flame—children of the Light who believe that the last word spoken over creation will not be sorrow, but resurrection.

From Dust We Walk Together

Kay Dennis

Monday of the Fifth Week of Lent — The Grain of Wheat

John 12:20–26 (NRSV)

Now among those who went up to worship at the festival were some Greeks. They came to Philip, who was from Bethsaida in Galilee, and said to him, "Sir, we wish to see Jesus." Philip went and told Andrew; then Andrew and Philip went and told Jesus. Jesus answered them, "The hour has come for the Son of Man to be glorified. Very truly, I tell you, unless a grain of wheat falls into the earth and dies, it remains just a single grain; but if it dies, it bears much fruit. Those who love their life lose it, and those who hate their life in this world will keep it for eternal life. Whoever serves me must follow me, and where I am, there will my servant be also. Whoever serves me, the Father will honor."

Reflection

Hope begins in hidden places. Jesus speaks these words on the eve of His passion, knowing that His followers cannot yet understand what glory through death means. They expect triumph; He promises transformation. A seed must fall, must be buried in darkness, before life bursts forth again.

The image of the grain of wheat is the paradox at the heart of Christian hope: life through loss, joy through surrender, abundance through dying. The world tells us to preserve ourselves at all costs, but Christ reveals a different kind of preservation—the eternal life that grows when we let go of control and entrust ourselves to God's soil.

This dying is not morbid resignation; it is the creative rhythm of divine love. Every act of generosity, every forgiveness offered, every comfort given to another is a kind of burial—a planting of self for the sake of something greater. Communities that live by this pattern become fields of grace.

In Lent we practice this surrender so that resurrection will not surprise us—it will recognize us. The hope of the gospel is not that death will be avoided, but that nothing given in love will ever be wasted. Every buried seed is already cradled in promise.

Prayer

O Christ, our Sower and our Harvest,
who teaches us that life is born of loss:
Plant Your hope deep within our hearts,
that dying to self, we may rise to serve You and one another

in the fullness of Your resurrection life;
through Jesus Christ our Lord. Amen.

Community Practice

Plant something small today—a seed, a bulb, or even a cutting from a plant. As you cover it with soil, pray that God will use your hidden acts of kindness to bear fruit for the world. Hope often begins where no one can see.

From Dust We Walk Together

Kay Dennis

Tuesday of the Fifth Week of Lent — The Valley of Dry Bones

Ezekiel 37:1–10 (NRSV)

The hand of the Lord came upon me, and he brought me out by the spirit of the Lord and set me down in the middle of a valley; it was full of bones. He led me all around them; there were very many lying in the valley, and they were very dry. He said to me, "Mortal, can these bones live?" I answered, "O Lord God, you know." Then he said to me, "Prophesy to these bones, and say to them: O dry bones, hear the word of the Lord. Thus says the Lord God to these bones: I will cause breath to enter you, and you shall live. I will lay sinews on you, and will cause flesh to come upon you, and cover you with skin, and put breath in you, and you shall live; and you shall know that I am the Lord."

So I prophesied as I had been commanded; and as I prophesied, suddenly there was a noise, a rattling, and the bones came together, bone to its bone. I looked, and there were sinews on them, and flesh had come upon them, and skin had covered them; but there was no breath in them. Then he said to me, "Prophesy to the breath, prophesy, mortal, and say to the breath: Thus says the Lord God: Come from the four winds, O breath, and breathe upon these slain, that they may live." I prophesied as he commanded me, and the breath came into them, and they lived, and stood on their feet, a vast multitude.

Reflection

There are few images in Scripture as haunting or as hopeful as this one. A valley full of bones—dry, scattered, beyond repair—and yet God asks the impossible question: "Can these bones live?" Ezekiel answers with the only honest faith possible in such a place: "O Lord God, you know."

This scene is not just about physical resurrection; it is about communal renewal. Israel's hope has collapsed, their identity shattered by exile. The bones represent a people who believe they are beyond restoration. But God calls Ezekiel to speak—not his own optimism, but the Word of the Lord. Hope begins to rattle when faith dares to speak life where death has reigned.

Notice the two movements of this miracle: first the bones come together, then breath enters them. Structure and spirit. Organization and inspiration. A community restored by God must have both—a shared framework and the living breath of the Spirit. Without the latter, even perfect order remains lifeless.

In every age, the Church finds itself in valleys of discouragement, wondering if its bones can live again. Lent assures us they can. The same Spirit that stirred

Ezekiel's valley is still at work, breathing life into our parched faith and weary institutions, calling us to stand again as a vast, living multitude of hope.

Prayer

O Breath of God,
who speaks life into what is dead and forgotten:
Breathe upon the dry bones of our hearts and our communities,
that we may rise, renewed in hope and strong in Your Spirit,
to proclaim Your living power in all the earth;
through Jesus Christ our Lord. Amen.

Community Practice

Visit a place that feels forgotten—a neglected cemetery, an abandoned building, a quiet corner of your town—and pray there. Ask God to bring renewal, not only to that place, but to all who have lost the breath of hope.

From Dust We Walk Together

Kay Dennis

Wednesday of the Fifth Week of Lent — Those Who Wait for the Lord

Isaiah 40:28–31 (NRSV)

> Have you not known? Have you not heard?
> The Lord is the everlasting God,
> the Creator of the ends of the earth.
> He does not faint or grow weary;
> his understanding is unsearchable.
> He gives power to the faint,
> and strengthens the powerless.
> Even youths will faint and be weary,
> and the young will fall exhausted;
> but those who wait for the Lord shall renew their strength,
> they shall mount up with wings like eagles,
> they shall run and not be weary,
> they shall walk and not faint.

Reflection

Isaiah's words fall like rain on tired souls. His audience—an exiled, despairing people—has almost forgotten what strength feels like. They are bone-weary of waiting for deliverance, exhausted from hope deferred. Into that fatigue comes this resounding reminder: "The Lord does not faint or grow weary."

Hope, Isaiah tells us, is not the denial of exhaustion; it is endurance through it. To "wait for the Lord" does not mean to sit passively but to lean into trust—to stretch the heart toward the horizon where God's promise dawns. The waiting itself becomes a form of faith, a quiet refusal to believe that despair has the last word.

We often think of eagles as soaring effortlessly above the storm, but they rise precisely because of the storm's wind. So it is with divine strength: it does not remove our trials, but lifts us through them. The faint become strong not by willpower but by grace—the exchange of human limitation for divine perseverance.

Communities, too, are renewed when they learn this rhythm of waiting together. Shared patience becomes shared strength. The church that prays through weariness, that holds one another through silence and uncertainty, learns to fly as one flock on the updraft of hope.

Kay Dennis

Prayer

Everlasting God,
whose strength never falters and whose mercy never ends:
Teach us to wait upon You with trusting hearts,
that we may rise on the wings of Your Spirit,
run the race of faith without weariness,
> and walk in steadfast hope;
> through Jesus Christ our Lord. Amen.

Community Practice

Reach out to someone who seems tired in body or spirit. Offer a word of encouragement, a helping hand, or simply your presence. When one person's wings falter, another's support can keep hope aloft.

From Dust We Walk Together

Kay Dennis

Thursday of the Fifth Week of Lent — A Future and a Hope

Jeremiah 29:10–14 (NRSV)

For thus says the Lord: Only when Babylon's seventy years are completed will I visit you, and I will fulfill to you my promise and bring you back to this place. For surely I know the plans I have for you, says the Lord, plans for your welfare and not for harm, to give you a future with hope. Then when you call upon me and come and pray to me, I will hear you. When you search for me, you will find me; if you seek me with all your heart, I will let you find me, says the Lord, and I will restore your fortunes and gather you from all the nations and all the places where I have driven you, says the Lord, and I will bring you back to the place from which I sent you into exile.

Reflection

This passage is one of Scripture's most beloved promises—but also one of its most misunderstood. The people who first heard Jeremiah's words were not celebrating a bright new beginning. They were living in exile, surrounded by uncertainty, far from home. God's "plans for a future and a hope" were spoken not into comfort, but into captivity.

Real hope is not a shortcut; it is a long obedience in the same direction. God's timeline unfolds through seasons we would rather skip—waiting, rebuilding, forgiving, starting over. Yet through it all, God's intention remains unwavering: welfare, not harm; future, not futility.

Notice that hope is tied not to escape but to relationship. "When you call upon me… when you search for me with all your heart." The restoration promised here is not just geographic—it is spiritual. God's people will return home not only to their land, but to their God.

In community, this kind of hope becomes contagious. One believer's endurance strengthens another's. A single heart that still dares to pray in exile can awaken a whole people to trust again. The plans of God may unfold slowly, but they never fail. The future of hope is already taking shape in the prayers of the present.

Prayer

Faithful God,
whose promises outlast every exile and every fear:
Renew our trust in Your providence,
that seeking You with all our hearts,
we may discover the hope that no captivity can destroy;
through Jesus Christ our Lord. Amen.

Kay Dennis

Community Practice

Write a letter—or even a simple note—to someone who feels far from home, whether literally or spiritually. Remind them that God's plans still include them, that their story is not over, and that hope is already on its way.

From Dust We Walk Together

Kay Dennis

Friday of the Fifth Week of Lent — Those Who Sow in Tears

Psalm 126 (NRSV)

> When the Lord restored the fortunes of Zion,
> we were like those who dream.
> Then our mouth was filled with laughter,
> and our tongue with shouts of joy;
> then it was said among the nations,
> "The Lord has done great things for them."
> The Lord has done great things for us,
> and we rejoiced.
>
> Restore our fortunes, O Lord,
> like the watercourses in the Negeb.
> May those who sow in tears
> reap with shouts of joy.
> Those who go out weeping,
> bearing the seed for sowing,
> shall come home with shouts of joy,
> carrying their sheaves.*

Reflection

This psalm captures the rhythm of redemption—memory and longing, joy and tears, past grace, and future hope. It begins as a song of celebration: "The Lord has done great things for us." But by the next verse, the singer is pleading again: "Restore our fortunes, O Lord." Joy and yearning coexist here, as they so often do in the life of faith.

"Those who sow in tears" is one of the most tender images in Scripture. It acknowledges that the work of hope often begins in sorrow. The soil of renewal is watered first by lament. Yet the psalm assures us that no tear is wasted—each one becomes a seed. When offered to God, our grief can germinate into compassion, our pain into promise.

The Negeb, a desert region in southern Israel, rarely sees rain; but when it does, dry riverbeds suddenly rush with life. So too, the arid seasons of our souls can surprise us with unexpected floods of grace. Hope does not erase sorrow; it redeems it. What is planted in suffering will one day return in joy.

In community, this psalm becomes a chorus of faith: one person sings from memory, another from longing, another from tears—and together they form the sound of restoration. The Church becomes a field of promise, waiting for the harvest only God can bring.

Kay Dennis

Prayer

God of our joy and our tears,
who turns mourning into dancing and sorrow into song:
Receive the seeds of our grief,
and by Your Spirit bring forth a harvest of hope,
that we may rejoice again in the land of Your mercy;
through Jesus Christ our Lord. Amen.

Community Practice

If you know someone walking through a difficult season, reach out with compassion. Offer a listening ear, a handwritten note, or a meal. Even small gestures can become seeds of hope that bloom later in ways unseen.

From Dust We Walk Together

Kay Dennis

Saturday of the Fifth Week of Lent — The Dawn Beyond the Cross

John 11:32–44 (NRSV)

When Mary came where Jesus was and saw him, she knelt at his feet and said to him, "Lord, if you had been here, my brother would not have died." When Jesus saw her weeping, and the Jews who came with her also weeping, he was greatly disturbed in spirit and deeply moved. He said, "Where have you laid him?" They said to him, "Lord, come and see." Jesus began to weep. So the Jews said, "See how he loved him!" But some of them said, "Could not he who opened the eyes of the blind man have kept this man from dying?"

Then Jesus, again greatly disturbed, came to the tomb. It was a cave, and a stone was lying against it. Jesus said, "Take away the stone." Martha, the sister of the dead man, said to him, "Lord, already there is a stench because he has been dead four days." Jesus said to her, "Did I not tell you that if you believed, you would see the glory of God?" So they took away the stone. And Jesus looked upward and said, "Father, I thank you for having heard me. I knew that you always hear me, but I have said this for the sake of the crowd standing here, so that they may believe that you sent me." When he had said this, he cried with a loud voice, "Lazarus, come out!" The dead man came out, his hands and feet bound with strips of cloth, and his face wrapped in a cloth. Jesus said to them, "Unbind him, and let him go."

Reflection

This moment stands on the edge between death and resurrection, grief, and glory. Before the empty tomb of Easter, there is the open tomb of Lazarus—a foreshadowing of hope that moves through tears, not around them.

Jesus weeps. The shortest verse in Scripture is also one of the most revealing. God does not stand at a distance from human sorrow; He enters it fully. The One who will soon conquer death first allows Himself to feel its sting. His tears are the bridge between divine power and human pain.

But the story does not end in lament. Christ commands, "Take away the stone," and with that act, hope becomes visible. Lazarus stumbles from the darkness, still bound, and Jesus instructs the community, "Unbind him, and let him go." Resurrection begins not only with God's voice but with human hands obeying it. The miracle is shared.

Lent prepares us for this dawning light—the promise that no grave, no loss, no despair can hold us forever. The same voice that called Lazarus still calls us by name, bidding us leave behind our burial cloths of fear and step into the morning of God's mercy. Beyond every cross, there is dawn.

Prayer

O Christ of tears and triumph,
who weeps at our tombs and calls us to rise:
Speak again Your word of life into our darkness,
and grant us grace to help unbind others,
that together we may walk into the dawn of Your glory;
who lives and reigns with the Father and the Holy Spirit,
one God, now and for ever. Amen.

Community Practice

Spend a few quiet minutes today remembering someone who has experienced loss—whether recent or long past. Light a candle in their honor, and pray that they (and you) may feel the tender presence of Christ who still weeps and still calls us into life.

From Dust We Walk Together

Kay Dennis

Saturday of the Fifth Week of Lent — The Dawn Beyond the Cross

John 11:32–44 (NRSV)

When Mary came where Jesus was and saw him, she knelt at his feet and said to him, "Lord, if you had been here, my brother would not have died." When Jesus saw her weeping, and the Jews who came with her also weeping, he was greatly disturbed in spirit and deeply moved. He said, "Where have you laid him?" They said to him, "Lord, come and see." Jesus began to weep. So the Jews said, "See how he loved him!" But some of them said, "Could not he who opened the eyes of the blind man have kept this man from dying?"

Then Jesus, again greatly disturbed, came to the tomb. It was a cave, and a stone was lying against it. Jesus said, "Take away the stone." Martha, the sister of the dead man, said to him, "Lord, already there is a stench because he has been dead four days." Jesus said to her, "Did I not tell you that if you believed, you would see the glory of God?" So they took away the stone. And Jesus looked upward and said, "Father, I thank you for having heard me. I knew that you always hear me, but I have said this for the sake of the crowd standing here, so that they may believe that you sent me." When he had said this, he cried with a loud voice, "Lazarus, come out!" The dead man came out, his hands and feet bound with strips of cloth, and his face wrapped in a cloth. Jesus said to them, "Unbind him, and let him go."

Reflection

This moment stands on the edge between death and resurrection, grief, and glory. Before the empty tomb of Easter, there is the open tomb of Lazarus—a foreshadowing of hope that moves through tears, not around them.

Jesus weeps. The shortest verse in Scripture is also one of the most revealing. God does not stand at a distance from human sorrow; He enters it fully. The One who will soon conquer death first allows Himself to feel its sting. His tears are the bridge between divine power and human pain.

But the story does not end in lament. Christ commands, "Take away the stone," and with that act, hope becomes visible. Lazarus stumbles from the darkness, still bound, and Jesus instructs the community, "Unbind him, and let him go." Resurrection begins not only with God's voice but with human hands obeying it. The miracle is shared.

Lent prepares us for this dawning light—the promise that no grave, no loss, no despair can hold us forever. The same voice that called Lazarus still calls us by name, bidding us leave behind our burial cloths of fear and step into the morning of God's mercy. Beyond every cross, there is dawn.

Prayer

O Christ of tears and triumph,
who weeps at our tombs and Callahan us to rise:
Speak again Your word of life into our darkness,
and grant us grace to help unbind others,
that together we may walk into the dawn of Your glory;
who lives and reigns with the Father and the Holy Spirit,
one God, now and for ever. Amen.

Community Practice

Spend a few quiet minutes today remembering someone who has experienced loss—whether recent or long past. Light a candle in their honor, and pray that they (and you) may feel the tender presence of Christ who still weeps and still calls us into life.

From Dust We Walk Together

Kay Dennis

The Fifth Sunday of Lent — The Hope That Does Not Disappoint

Romans 5:1–5 (NRSV)

Therefore, since we are justified by faith, we have peace with God through our Lord Jesus Christ, through whom we have obtained access to this grace in which we stand; and we boast in our hope of sharing the glory of God. And not only that, but we also boast in our sufferings, knowing that suffering produces endurance, and endurance produces character, and character produces hope, and hope does not disappoint us, because God's love has been poured into our hearts through the Holy Spirit that has been given to us.

Reflection

Hope is not wishful thinking—it is the fruit of endurance. Paul writes these words to a community that knows hardship intimately, and yet he insists that suffering, when held in grace, becomes the soil where true hope grows. Not because pain itself is good, but because God's love refuses to waste it.

There is a sequence here: suffering → endurance → character → hope. Each step shapes the heart to hold more of God's presence. The path of faith does not bypass hardship; it redeems it. The same Spirit that poured love into our hearts at the beginning of the journey continues to pour it still, filling the cracks created by struggle until we overflow again.

To "boast in our sufferings" sounds strange until we remember that Paul is not glorifying pain—he is glorifying God's constancy within it. The cross stands at the center of this truth. Christ's own suffering did not end in despair but in resurrection, turning the world's greatest wound into its greatest hope.

Communities that walk through sorrow together are the truest witnesses of this gospel. They know, from lived experience, that hope born of love cannot disappoint. Such hope does not depend on outcomes but on presence—the assurance that nothing, not even death, can separate us from the love of God in Christ Jesus.

Prayer

God of steadfast love,
who brings peace out of pain and life out of death:
Pour Your Spirit anew into our hearts,
that in every trial we may find strength,
in every sorrow endurance,
and in every cross the unbreakable hope of resurrection;
through Jesus Christ our Lord. Amen.

Kay Dennis

Community Practice

Gather with a few others—friends, family, or members of your church—and share stories of a time you have seen hope emerge from hardship. Listen for the common thread of God's love woven through them all. End your time by giving thanks together for the Spirit who never abandons us.

From Dust We Walk Together

Kay Dennis

Looking Ahead — Together at the Cross

We have come far on this Lenten road—through dust and trust, through thirst and light, through hope that grows in hidden soil. Each step has brought us closer to the center of the story, the place where all our paths converge: the cross.

To stand together at the cross is to face both the world's sorrow and God's steadfast love. It is to see, in one piercing moment, how the worst of human cruelty meets the fullness of divine mercy. Hope, it turns out, is not born in comfort but in compassion—in the God who enters our suffering and transforms it from within.

At the cross, all illusions fall away. Power gives way to vulnerability. Judgment yields to forgiveness. Death is unmasked as the doorway to life. Here, hope becomes more than sentiment—it becomes salvation. What began in ashes now glows with a light that the darkness cannot overcome.

As we enter Holy Week, we do not walk alone. We carry one another's prayers, stories, and small resurrections. Together we approach the hill called Calvary, not as spectators but as those who have learned to hope in the midst of sorrow. Beyond the cross waits dawn—the dawn that remakes the world.

From Dust We Walk Together

Kay Dennis

Palm Sunday — The Road That Leads to Love

Luke 19:28–40 (NRSV)

After he had said this, he went on ahead, going up to Jerusalem. When he had come near Bethphage and Bethany, at the place called the Mount of Olives, he sent two of the disciples, saying, "Go into the village ahead of you, and as you enter it you will find tied there a colt that has never been ridden. Untie it and bring it here. If anyone asks you, 'Why are you untying it?' just say this, 'The Lord needs it.'"

So those who were sent departed and found it as he had told them. As they were untying the colt, its owners asked them, "Why are you untying the colt?" They said, "The Lord needs it." Then they brought it to Jesus; and after throwing their cloaks on the colt, they set Jesus on it. As he rode along, people kept spreading their cloaks on the road. As he was now approaching the path down from the Mount of Olives, the whole multitude of the disciples began to praise God joyfully with a loud voice for all the deeds of power that they had seen, saying, "Blessed is the king who comes in the name of the Lord! Peace in heaven, and glory in the highest heaven!" Some of the Pharisees in the crowd said to him, "Teacher, order your disciples to stop." He answered, "I tell you, if these were silent, the stones would shout out."

Reflection

The road to Jerusalem is lined with shouts of joy and seeds of sorrow. The same voices crying "Hosanna!" will soon echo with "Crucify him!" And yet Jesus does not turn back. He rides on—humble, unarmed, vulnerable—embodying a kingship that looks nothing like the world's power.

Every detail of this entry is charged with paradox. The colt is borrowed, the crowd is ordinary, and the triumph is fleeting. But the love it reveals is eternal. The road that begins in celebration ends in sacrifice, and yet both are woven from the same thread of divine compassion. Christ knows what awaits Him, and still He rides toward the city, not in defiance but in mercy.

Palm Sunday is the threshold of holy tension—rejoicing and foreboding intertwined. It reminds us that love will go wherever we will not, that grace is not afraid of the streets where betrayal hides in the crowd. The stones themselves are ready to sing because creation knows what we forget: that true kingship is service, true victory is surrender, and true power is love willing to die.

Kay Dennis

Prayer

O Christ, our King of peace,
who rides not upon a warhorse but upon a borrowed colt:
Teach us the way of Your humility,
that following You in the path of love,
we may bear Your peace into the streets of a restless world;
who lives and reigns with the Father and the Holy Spirit,
one God, now and for ever. Amen.

Community Practice

Take a walk today through your neighborhood or town. As you walk, pray silently for the people who live and work along your path. Offer each step as a small act of peace—your own "procession" of love into the world.

Monday in Holy Week — The Fragrance of Love

John 12:1–8 (NRSV)

Six days before the Passover Jesus came to Bethany, the home of Lazarus, whom he had raised from the dead.

There they gave a dinner for him. Martha served, and Lazarus was one of those at the table with him. Mary took a pound of costly perfume made of pure nard, anointed Jesus' feet, and wiped them with her hair. The house was filled with the fragrance of the perfume. But Judas Iscariot, one of his disciples (the one who was about to betray him), said, "Why was this perfume not sold for three hundred denarii and the money given to the poor?" (He said this not because he cared about the poor, but because he was a thief; he kept the common purse and used to steal what was put into it.) Jesus said, "Leave her alone. She bought it so that she might keep it for the day of my burial. You always have the poor with you, but you do not always have me."

Reflection

The story opens not in a temple or a crowd, but at a dinner table—an ordinary moment transformed by extravagant devotion. Mary breaks open a jar of perfume worth a year's wages and pours it over Jesus' feet. The gesture is shocking, intimate, and tender. It is also prophetic. Without fully realizing it, she anoints Him for burial.

The fragrance fills the house, lingering long after her act is done. Love always leaves a scent—it lingers in memory, in the air of a home, in the hearts of those who witness it. But not everyone recognizes its beauty. Judas calls it wasteful, impractical. The contrast between the two is not only about greed; it is about vision. Mary sees with the eyes of love what others cannot yet grasp—that the cross is coming, and this moment is her offering before the shadow falls.

Every act of love given freely is a kind of anointing. It prepares the world for resurrection. In this scene, hope takes the form of perfume poured out, beauty that seems wasted but is never lost. The house of faith still carries its fragrance.

Prayer

O Lord of love and loss,
who was anointed for death by the hands of a friend:
Teach us to pour out the perfume of our devotion without counting the cost,
that the fragrance of our love may fill the world with Your presence;
through Jesus Christ our Lord. Amen.

Community Practice

Do something generous and beautiful today that no one expects—give a gift, offer time, write a note of gratitude. Let the act itself become your perfume, released not for recognition, but for love.

From Dust We Walk Together

Kay Dennis

Tuesday in Holy Week — The Grain Falls to the Earth

John 12:23–33 (NRSV)

Jesus answered them, "The hour has come for the Son of Man to be glorified. Very truly, I tell you, unless a grain of wheat falls into the earth and dies, it remains just a single grain; but if it dies, it bears much fruit. Those who love their life lose it, and those who hate their life in this world will keep it for eternal life. Whoever serves me must follow me, and where I am, there will my servant be also. Whoever serves me, the Father will honor."

"Now my soul is troubled. And what should I say—'Father, save me from this hour'? No, it is for this reason that I have come to this hour. Father, glorify your name." Then a voice came from heaven, "I have glorified it, and I will glorify it again." The crowd standing there heard it and said that it was thunder. Others said, "An angel has spoken to him." Jesus answered, "This voice has come for your sake, not for mine. Now is the judgment of this world; now the ruler of this world will be driven out. And I, when I am lifted up from the earth, will draw all people to myself." He said this to indicate the kind of death he was to die.

Reflection

The seed has appeared before—the grain of wheat that must fall and die to bear fruit. But now, on the threshold of the cross, the image takes on its full weight. The hour has come. The soil of redemption waits open, ready to receive the seed of divine love.

This is the paradox of glory in John's Gospel: exaltation through descent, life through death, victory through surrender. Jesus' troubled soul reveals the cost of such obedience. The grain does not fall without pain, but its falling is not futile. The harvest it yields is measured not in crops but in hearts drawn to God.

"And I, when I am lifted up… will draw all people to myself." The magnetism of the cross is at once mysterious and universal. It gathers everything—sorrow, guilt, beauty, despair—into the gravity of divine compassion. No one is left outside its reach.

In our own lives, every act of surrender—every letting go of control, every death to ego—becomes a small participation in this mystery. Lent has been preparing us for this truth: that to follow Christ is to allow love to bury us deeply enough that resurrection can take root. Hope begins to sprout where the soil has been broken.

Kay Dennis

Prayer

O Christ, Seed of eternal life,
who fell into the earth that we might live:
Teach us to follow You through surrender into fruitfulness,
that dying to self,
we may rise to bear Your harvest of love in the world;
who lives and reigns with the Father and the Holy Spirit,
one God, now and for ever. Amen.

Community Practice

Spend time outdoors today, if possible. Hold a seed or a handful of soil. Reflect on how God brings life from what seems dead and unseen. Pray that your own life may be fertile ground for the growth of grace in others.

From Dust We Walk Together

Kay Dennis

Wednesday in Holy Week — Betrayal in the Night

John 13:21–30 (NRSV)

After saying this Jesus was troubled in spirit, and declared, "Very truly, I tell you, one of you will betray me." The disciples looked at one another, uncertain of whom he was speaking. One of his disciples—the one whom Jesus loved—was reclining next to him; Simon Peter therefore motioned to him to ask Jesus of whom he was speaking. So while reclining next to Jesus, he asked him, "Lord, who is it?" Jesus answered, "It is the one to whom I give this piece of bread when I have dipped it in the dish." So when he had dipped the piece of bread, he gave it to Judas son of Simon Iscariot. After he received the piece of bread, Satan entered into him. Jesus said to him, "Do quickly what you are going to do." Now no one at the table knew why he said this to him. Some thought that, because Judas had the common purse, Jesus was telling him, "Buy what we need for the festival;" or, that he should give something to the poor. So, after receiving the piece of bread, he immediately went out. And it was night.

Reflection

Few words in Scripture fall heavier than these: "And it was night." The darkness is not only around them—it is within them. Jesus, the Light of the world, is surrounded by shadows of confusion, fear, and betrayal. Yet even here, love does not retreat.

Before Judas leaves, Jesus offers him bread—an act of hospitality and friendship. This final gesture is one last appeal of grace. It is as if Jesus says, "Even now, I feed you." The hand of mercy reaches out to the hand that will betray. There is no bitterness in Christ, only sorrow and steadfast compassion.

The betrayal of Judas is not so distant from our own hearts as we might wish. Every time we choose safety over truth, comfort over compassion, or self over love, we too step into the night. Yet the miracle of grace is this: even in betrayal, God is already working redemption. The darkness that Judas enters will soon hold the cross—and in that cross, the dawn will break again.

Lent brings us to this threshold honestly. We cannot follow Jesus without acknowledging the night within and around us. But we need not fear it. For the One who enters the night does not lose His way; He transforms it into morning.

Prayer

Kay Dennis

O Christ, Light in our darkness,
who loved even those who betrayed You:
Keep us steadfast when shadows fall,
and grant us courage to face our own darkness
until Your dawn restores us to love and to peace;
who lives and reigns with the Father and the Holy Spirit,
one God, now and for ever. Amen.

Community Practice

This evening, light a single candle and sit for a few minutes in the dark. Reflect on the ways you have felt distant from God or from others. Offer those moments honestly to Christ, trusting that His light still shines in your night.

From Dust We Walk Together

Kay Dennis

Maundy Thursday — The Basin and the Towel

John 13:1–15 (NRSV)

Now before the festival of the Passover, Jesus knew that his hour had come to depart from this world and go to the Father. Having loved his own who were in the world, he loved them to the end. The devil had already put it into the heart of Judas son of Simon Iscariot to betray him. And during supper Jesus, knowing that the Father had given all things into his hands, and that he had come from God and was going to God, got up from the table, took off his outer robe, and tied a towel around himself. Then he poured water into a basin and began to wash the disciples' feet and to wipe them with the towel that was tied around him.

He came to Simon Peter, who said to him, "Lord, are you going to wash my feet?" Jesus answered, "You do not know now what I am doing, but later you will understand." Peter said to him, "You will never wash my feet." Jesus answered, "Unless I wash you, you have no share with me." Simon Peter said to him, "Lord, not my feet only but also my hands and my head!" Jesus said to him, "One who has bathed does not need to wash, except for the feet, but is entirely clean. And you are clean, though not all of you." For he knew who was to betray him; for this reason he said, "Not all of you are clean."

After he had washed their feet, had put on his robe, and had returned to the table, he said to them, "Do you know what I have done to you? You call me Teacher and Lord—and you are right, for that is what I am. So if I, your Lord and Teacher, have washed your feet, you also ought to wash one another's feet. For I have set you an example, that you also should do as I have done to you."

Reflection

The night before His death, Jesus does not take up a sword or a crown. He takes up a towel. The One who shaped the stars now kneels to wash the dust from His disciples' feet. It is an act so humble, so startling, that Peter can hardly bear it. Yet this is what divine love looks like in human form—kneeling, cleansing, serving.

John tells us that Jesus "knew that the Father had given all things into His hands." And what does He do with that authority? He uses those same hands to wash feet. The basin becomes His throne, the towel His scepter. In this inversion, the meaning of power itself is rewritten.

To wash another's feet is to enter the space of vulnerability—both for the one serving and the one being served. Peter resists because it feels too intimate, too equal. But Jesus insists that we must receive love before we can offer it. Only those who have been washed by grace can wash others in humility.

Maundy Thursday's commandment—"Love one another as I have loved you"—is not sentimental. It is revolutionary. It calls the Church to a love willing to kneel, to serve, and to risk being misunderstood. The basin and the towel remain our truest emblems of discipleship.

Prayer

Servant Lord,
who took the towel and the basin and washed the feet of Your own:
Cleanse us from pride and fear,
that we may learn to love as You have loved us,
and in humility serve one another for Your sake;
who lives and reigns with the Father and the Holy Spirit,
one God, now and for ever. Amen.

Community Practice

If possible, wash another's hands or feet today—literally or symbolically. Offer to help someone with a small, humble task: cleaning, cooking, carrying, or listening. Let every act of service become a quiet echo of the love that knelt in the upper room.

From Dust We Walk Together

Kay Dennis

Good Friday — The Love That Will Not Let Go

John 19:16–30 (NRSV)

So they took Jesus; and carrying the cross by himself, he went out to what is called The Place of the Skull, which in Hebrew is called Golgotha. There they crucified him, and with him two others, one on either side, with Jesus between them. Pilate also had an inscription written and put on the cross. It read, "Jesus of Nazareth, the King of the Jews." Many of the Jews read this inscription because the place where Jesus was crucified was near the city; and it was written in Hebrew, in Latin, and in Greek.

When the soldiers had crucified Jesus, they took his clothes and divided them into four parts, one for each soldier. They also took his tunic; now the tunic was seamless, woven in one piece from the top. So they said to one another, "Let us not tear it, but cast lots for it to see who will get it." This was to fulfill what the scripture says,

"They divided my clothes among themselves,
and for my clothing they cast lots."
And that is what the soldiers did.

Meanwhile, standing near the cross of Jesus were his mother, and his mother's sister, Mary the wife of Clopas, and Mary Magdalene. When Jesus saw his mother and the disciple whom he loved standing beside her, he said to his mother, "Woman, here is your son." Then he said to the disciple, "Here is your mother." And from that hour the disciple took her into his own home.

After this, when Jesus knew that all was now finished, he said (in order to fulfill the scripture), "I am thirsty." A jar full of sour wine was standing there. So they put a sponge full of the wine on a branch of hyssop and held it to his mouth. When Jesus had received the wine, he said, "It is finished." Then he bowed his head and gave up his spirit.

Reflection

The cross is the center of all things. Here the story of humanity reaches both its lowest depth and its highest grace. Every betrayal, every cruelty, every grief converges on this hill—and is met, not with vengeance, but with love that will not let go.

Jesus carries the cross alone, yet He is never more united with the world. The inscription above His head declares His kingship in every language, as if creation itself must bear witness. Around Him are soldiers gambling, friends hiding, and His mother weeping. Still, from the cross He speaks—not words of rage, but of relationship: "Here is your son... Here is your mother." Even in agony, He builds community.

When He says, "It is finished," it is not a cry of defeat. It is the triumphant declaration of completion—the fulfillment of love's long labor. The work of redemption is whole. The curtain is torn, the barrier gone. The God who entered flesh has carried human suffering to its very end and transformed it from the inside out.

On this day, we stand before the cross not as spectators but as the beloved for whom He died. We bring our darkness, our despair, our fractured world—and hear in return the steady heartbeat of mercy. The Light has entered the night and will not be extinguished.

Prayer

O Crucified Lord,
whose arms were stretched upon the cross to embrace the world:
Hold us in Your mercy when we face the darkness of our own making,
that we may know Your forgiveness and share Your compassion
until the dawn of resurrection;
who lives and reigns with the Father and the Holy Spirit,
one God, for ever and ever. Amen.

Community Practice

Spend time today in silence. Turn off distractions. If possible, sit before a cross or an image of it. Let the stillness speak. Reflect on the places in your life and in the world that most need the healing power of Christ's love—and place them, one by one, at the foot of the cross.

Kay Dennis

Holy Saturday — The Silence Between

Matthew 27:57–66 (NRSV)

When it was evening, there came a rich man from Arimathea, named Joseph, who was also a disciple of Jesus. He went to Pilate and asked for the body of Jesus; then Pilate ordered it to be given to him. So Joseph took the body and wrapped it in a clean linen cloth and laid it in his own new tomb, which he had hewn in the rock. He then rolled a great stone to the door of the tomb and went away. Mary Magdalene and the other Mary were there, sitting opposite the tomb.

The next day, that is, after the day of Preparation, the chief priests and the Pharisees gathered before Pilate and said, "Sir, we remember what that impostor said while he was still alive, 'After three days I will rise again.' Therefore command the tomb to be made secure until the third day; otherwise his disciples may go and steal him away, and tell the people, 'He has been raised from the dead,' and the last deception would be worse than the first." Pilate said to them, "You have a guard of soldiers; go, make it as secure as you can." So they went with the guard and made the tomb secure by sealing the stone.

Reflection

Holy Saturday is the day between—the stillness that holds both grief and promise. The cross has fallen silent. The tomb is sealed. Heaven seems quiet. Creation itself pauses, as though holding its breath.

Joseph's careful act of devotion, wrapping and laying the body of Jesus in the tomb, is love persevering when hope appears lost. The women sitting opposite the tomb teach us the same lesson: sometimes the holiest thing we can do is simply remain. When words fail, presence becomes prayer.

This day is the hinge of the world—the space between death and life, despair, and resurrection. It is a day that many of us know too well: the long waiting after loss, the uncertainty between the breaking and the healing. Yet even in this silence, God is at work. Hidden beneath the surface of sorrow, resurrection is already stirring.

The Church keeps this day not to dwell in darkness, but to honor the mystery that even in the grave, love is not idle. The stillness of Holy Saturday is not emptiness; it is gestation. The seed planted in the earth on Good Friday begins to quicken. Soon the stone will roll, and the garden will awaken.

Kay Dennis

Prayer

O God of silence and of promise,
who dwells in the shadows of the tomb and the depths of the heart:
Teach us to wait with faith when light seems gone,
to trust that Your love is never still,
and to rest in the hope of resurrection yet unseen;
through Jesus Christ our Lord. Amen.

Community Practice

Keep a portion of this day in silence. Turn off music, television, or noise. Sit in quiet awareness of God's presence. Let the stillness speak of what words cannot: that even when all seems finished, love continues its hidden work.

From Dust We Walk Together

Kay Dennis

Easter Sunday — The Dawn of All Dawns

John 20:1–18 (NRSV)

Early on the first day of the week, while it was still dark, Mary Magdalene came to the tomb and saw that the stone had been removed from the tomb. So she ran and went to Simon Peter and the other disciple, the one whom Jesus loved, and said to them, "They have taken the Lord out of the tomb, and we do not know where they have laid him." Then Peter and the other disciple set out and went toward the tomb.

The two were running together, but the other disciple outran Peter and reached the tomb first. He bent down to look in and saw the linen wrappings lying there, but he did not go in. Then Simon Peter came, following him, and went into the tomb. He saw the linen wrappings lying there, and the cloth that had been on Jesus' head, not lying with the linen wrappings but rolled up in a place by itself. Then the other disciple, who reached the tomb first, also went in, and he saw and believed; for as yet they did not understand the scripture, that he must rise from the dead. Then the disciples returned to their homes.

But Mary stood weeping outside the tomb. As she wept, she bent over to look into the tomb; and she saw two angels in white, sitting where the body of Jesus had been lying, one at the head and the other at the feet. They said to her, "Woman, why are you weeping?" She said to them, "They have taken away my Lord, and I do not know where they have laid him." When she had said this, she turned around and saw Jesus standing there, but she did not know that it was Jesus. Jesus said to her, "Woman, why are you weeping? Whom are you looking for?" Supposing him to be the gardener, she said to him, "Sir, if you have carried him away, tell me where you have laid him, and I will take him away." Jesus said to her, "Mary!" She turned and said to him in Hebrew, "Rabbouni!" (which means Teacher). Jesus said to her, "Do not hold on to me, because I have not yet ascended to the Father. But go to my brothers and say to them, 'I am ascending to my Father and your Father, to my God and your God.'" Mary Magdalene went and announced to the disciples, "I have seen the Lord"; and she told them that he had said these things to her.

Reflection

The first word of Easter is not thunder or triumph—it is a name. "Mary." In the garden's quiet dawn, the risen Christ calls her as a shepherd calls His sheep, and everything changes. What began in darkness ends in recognition. The silence of Holy Saturday gives way to the voice of love alive again.

    Easter does not erase the cross; it fulfills it. The wounds remain, yet they no longer speak of death—they shine with glory. The garden becomes the new creation, the place where sorrow and joy embrace. Resurrection is not a metaphor; it is the miracle of God's own life bursting into the world again.

Mary becomes the first preacher of this good news, the apostle to the apostles. Her tears become testimony. Hope now has a name and a face. The same Christ who called Lazarus from the tomb now calls all creation to rise.

To live as Easter people is to carry resurrection wherever we go—to see life where others see loss, to proclaim love stronger than death, and to build community rooted in joy. The stone has been rolled away not only from His tomb, but from ours. The dawn of all dawns has begun.

Prayer

Risen Lord,
whose triumph over death has filled the world with light:
Call us by name as You called Mary,
that we may recognize You in our midst
and bear Your hope into every shadowed place;
who lives and reigns with the Father and the Holy Spirit,
one God, for ever and ever. Amen.

Community Practice

Greet this Easter morning as Mary did—with awe and joy. Step outside at dawn, breathe deeply, and whisper, "I have seen the Lord." Then share that hope with someone who needs to hear it today.

Kay Dennis

Sending Forth — The Work of Resurrection

The journey that began in dust now ends in dawn.

We have walked through wilderness and water, through thirst and light, through hope and sorrow, until at last we have stood before the empty tomb. Yet in truth, this is not the end of Lent—it is the beginning of resurrection life.

The season of repentance has opened into renewal; the silence of Holy Saturday has become the song of Easter morning. Still, the call remains: Go. Resurrection was never meant to be contained within a single garden or a single morning. It is meant to be carried—into kitchens and classrooms, hospitals and city streets, conversations, and quiet hearts.

To live as people of the Resurrection is to practice hope in ordinary ways:

    to forgive when bitterness feels easier,

    to listen when the world demands shouting,

    to mend what has been broken,

    to see Christ in the faces that others pass by.

It is to believe, even on weary days, that the stone is still rolling and the Light is still rising.

Easter is not a conclusion; it is a commission. The Risen Christ breathes peace upon His friends and sends them into the world to do the work of resurrection—

small, daily acts of courage and compassion that proclaim, "Love is stronger than death."

    So go now, children of dust and light.
    Walk gently upon this renewed earth.
    Carry the fragrance of grace wherever you go.
    Let your life be the hallelujah that never ends.

Kay Dennis

Benediction

May the God who formed you from the dust,
breathe into you again the Spirit of life.
May Christ, who walked the Lenten road,
walk beside you on every path of love and service.
And may the Holy Spirit, the flame of resurrection,
kindle in you such hope and joy
that all who meet you may glimpse the glory of God.

Go in peace to love and to serve,
and to proclaim with your life: Christ is risen. Alleluia.

Epigraph

"You are dust, and to dust you shall return."
— Genesis 3:19

"Yet the Lord God formed man from the dust of the ground,
and breathed into his nostrils the breath of life;
and the man became a living being."
— Genesis 2:7

"We, though many, are one body in Christ,
and individually we are members one of another."
— Romans 12:5

From Dust We Walk Together

Kay Dennis

Collect for Lent

"Almighty and everlasting God,
you hate nothing you have made
and forgive the sins of all who are penitent:
Create and make in us new and contrite hearts,
that we, worthily lamenting our sins
and acknowledging our wretchedness,
may obtain of you, the God of all mercy,
perfect remission and forgiveness;
through Jesus Christ our Lord,
who lives and reigns with you and the Holy Spirit,
one God, for ever and ever. Amen."
   (Book of Common Prayer, p. 217)

From Dust We Walk Together

Kay Dennis

Afterword — The Journey Continues

Lent has ended, but the life it points to has only begun.

The ashes have been brushed away, the alleluias restored, yet the work of resurrection continues in every act of love we dare to offer the world.

We have walked together through the wilderness—through sorrow, silence, and hope—and discovered along the way that God's mercy is not seasonal. It is steady, like breath. It waits in every dawn, every table, every act of kindness that whispers, "Christ is risen."

As this Lenten journey closes, may it open something new in you:

a gentler rhythm of prayer, a deeper sense of belonging,

a courage to love without counting the cost.

May you carry this season's lessons into ordinary days,

trusting that even now, the Spirit is at work—

breathing life into dust, knitting community from grace,

and turning every ending into the beginning of hope.

From Dust We Walk Together

Kay Dennis

Blessing for the Road

Go now, beloved dust,
into a world still hungry for resurrection.
Carry with you the breath of God,
the memory of the wilderness,
and the quiet knowing that love has already won.

May your hands become instruments of peace.
May your words mend what fear has broken.
May your feet walk paths of mercy,
and may your heart remain soft enough
to recognize Christ in every stranger's face.

Do not be afraid of ordinary days.
They are the altars where grace still gathers.
Listen for the Spirit in the laughter of neighbors,
in the prayers whispered over coffee,
in the stillness between one heartbeat and the next.

You are dust, yes—
but holy dust,
beloved and breathing,
shaped by the hands of the Creator
and called to bear the light of resurrection
wherever you go.

Go in peace.

From Dust We Walk Together

Go in love.
Go together.

Kay Dennis

//From Dust We Walk Together//

Note on the Scriptures

All Scripture quotations in this book are taken from the New Revised Standard Version Bible,
© National Council of the Churches of Christ in the U.S.A. Used by permission. All rights reserved.

Lectionary readings are based on the Book of Common Prayer (1979), following the appointed texts for Year A of the Revised Common Lectionary, adapted for use in Lent and Holy Week.

Kay Dennis

From Dust We Walk Together

Kay Dennis

Author's Note

This book was born in the in-between moments—between church bells and quiet mornings, between grief and grace, between the longing to draw closer to God and the hope of doing so together.

I have always loved the season of Lent for its honesty. It does not rush us toward joy, nor does it hide from sorrow. It simply invites us to walk—step by step, prayer by prayer—toward the truth that God meets us in our humanity. And in that meeting, we are changed.

The reflections that follow were written with community in mind. Each reading offers a piece of Scripture, a meditation, a prayer, and a small act to live out that day's grace. Some are meant to be shared aloud, others to be pondered in silence. All are invitations to remember that faith grows best not in perfection, but in presence—in showing up for God and for one another.

I have learned, again and again, that Lent is not about what we give up, but about what we make room for: the slow work of love, the rediscovery of hope, and the miracle of belonging. My prayer is that these pages will accompany you through the wilderness with gentleness, honesty, and light.

May you find in the dust not despair, but divine breath.

May you find, in community, the steady pulse of resurrection already beginning to rise.

From Dust We Walk Together

Kay Dennis

Acknowledgments

This book was written in the quiet spaces between seasons—in the hush before dawn, in the soft ache of Lent's waiting, and in the company of a faith community whose presence made every word possible.

To my fellow travelers in faith: thank you for walking this road together.

For every prayer whispered in hope, every hand extended in kindness, every story shared in honesty—you have shown me what resurrection looks like long before Easter morning.

To the Church that shaped me: your hymns, your silences, and your shared tables are woven through these pages. You have taught me that holiness is not found in isolation, but in belonging. May this book, in some small way, give back the grace you have given me.

To my bishop, mentors, teachers, and companions in ministry: thank you for reminding me that theology is lived most truthfully in service. Your wisdom and patience have been the scaffolding for every reflection here.

From Dust We Walk Together

To those who encouraged me to keep writing when the words felt too heavy—thank you.

To those who shared their stories of faith, doubt, and courage—you have lent this work its heart.

To my family—thank you for the grace you give so freely. For your patience when I disappeared into pages, for your kindness when words came slowly, and for your steady love that held me while this book was being written. This work is shaped by your presence more than you know.

To my husband—thank you for your love and unspoken sacrifices. You carried more than your share so that I could write, and you did so with patience, humor, and grace. This book bears the imprint of your faithfulness on every page.

And finally, and most importantly, to the God, my God, who gathers dust into community,
who breathes through frail hearts and builds from them a kingdom of light: all gratitude, all glory, all love be Yours.

Kay Dennis

About the Author

Kay Dennis is an ordained deacon is the Episcopal Diocese of the Central Gulf Coast and writer whose ministry lives at the intersection of faith, community, and story. Drawing from years of pastoral service and creative reflection, she invites readers to find God in the small, unguarded moments of daily life—where prayer meets the ordinary and grace grows quietly between neighbors.

When not writing, Kay can often be found walking with local congregations through the rhythms of worship, service, and hope, believing that the Church's truest strength is found in togetherness.

From Dust We Walk Together is her invitation to rediscover the sacred beauty of belonging—to God, to one another, and to the world God so loves.

From Dust We Walk Together

Kay Dennis

Other Books by the Author

Surviving Hurricane Michael

A moving chronicle of a community's endurance through the devastation of a Category Five hurricane—stories of loss, courage, faith, and the long road to recovery.

The Darkest Quest

A gripping psychological thriller that unravels the hidden world of human trafficking and the fragile hope that fights to survive in its shadows.

Candles in the Dark

A devotional-poetic journey through Advent and Christmas, celebrating the mystery of incarnation and the quiet ways love comes into the world.

Always: A Love through the Years

A book of poetry that traces a lifelong love shaped by time, loss, and perseverance, showing how devotion deepens rather than fades as years pass. It is a tender reflection on how love endures change, carries memory, and becomes a steady grace across a lifetime.

For information about upcoming works or speaking engagements, please contact the author through Kay.dennis@mail.com.

From Dust We Walk Together

Kay Dennis

Colophon

From Dusk We Walk Together: Reflections for the Lenten Journey
© 2026 by Kay Dennis
All rights reserved.

No part of this book may be reproduced, stored in a retrieval system, or transmitted in any form or by any means—electronic, mechanical, photocopying, recording, or otherwise—without prior written permission from the author, except for brief quotations used in reviews or academic study.

All Scripture quotations are from the New Revised Standard Version Bible,© National Council of the Churches of Christ in the U.S.A. Used by permission. All rights reserved.

Lectionary readings are based on the Book of Common Prayer (1979), according to the appointed texts for Year A of the Revised Common Lectionary.

Cover design and interior layout by Kay Dennis
Typography: Garamond 12 pt

Printed in the United States of America
10 9 8 7 6 5 4 3 2 1

From Dust We Walk Together

First Edition, 2026

Made in the USA
Coppell, TX
18 January 2026

69486418R00132